ENCYCLOPAEDIA OF INDIAN GOVERNMENT: PROGRAMMES AND POLICIES

ENCYCLOPAEDIA
OF
INDIAN GOVERNMENT:
PROGRAMMES AND POLICIES

Vol. 35

Communication Media

Edited by

Satish Tiwari

ANMOL PUBLICATIONS PVT. LTD.

NEW DELHI - 110 002 (INDIA)

ANMOL PUBLICATIONS PVT. LTD.
4374/4B, Ansari Road, Daryaganj
New Delhi - 110 002

Encyclopaedia of Indian Government: Programmes and Policies

First Edition, 2000
ISBN 81-261-0515-1 (Set)

PRINTED IN INDIA

Published by J.L. Kumar for Anmol Publications Pvt. Ltd., New Delhi - 110 002 and Printed at Mehra Offset Press, Delhi.

Contents

Preface

Encyclopaedia of Indian Government: Programmes and Policies contains authoritative information on about fifty departmental policies and their future developmental programmes.

Organised to be completed in 40 volumes, this gigantic work covers Agriculture; Atomic Energy; Chemicals and Fertilizers; Coal; Commerce; Communication; Culture; Defence; Education; Environment and Forests; External Affairs; Finance; Food & Consumer Affairs; Food Processing Industries; Health and Family Welfare; Home Affairs and Internal Security; Human Resources; Industry; Information and Broadcasting; Labour; Law, Justice and Company Affairs; Non-conventional Energy Sources; Ocean Development; Parliamentary Affairs; Personnel, Public Grievances and Pensions; Petroleum and Natural Gas; Planning and Programme Implementation; Planning and Statistics; Posts and Telegraphs; Power; Rural Development; Science and Technology; Social Justice and Empowerment; Space; States Affairs; Steel; Steel and Mines; Sugar and Edible Oils; Surface Transport; Textiles; Tourism; Urban Development; Water Resources; Women and Child development etc.

Based on the information derived from authoritative sources, this work contains authentic facts and figures. I am deeply beholden to all the scholars whose writings are cited or substantially made use of in the present work. I am also thankful to Anmol Publications Pvt. Ltd. for undertaking publication of this encyclopaedia. I am solely responsible for shortcomings in presentation of matter.

Encyclopaedic in nature, this will prove a dependable reference work for scholars and academics besides those appearing for different competitive examinations.

—Satish Tiwari

1

Introduction

Economic scenario

The year 1997-98 witnessed a growth rate in GDP of about 5 per cent, against a growth of 7.5 per cent in 1996-97. The average rate of growth of the economy rose from 6 per cent per annum in the seventh plan (1985-90) to 6.8 per cent per annum in eighth plan (1992-97). Growth averaged a high of 7.5 per cent per annum in the last three years (1994-97) of the eighth plan. The drop in GDP growth in 199798 is attributable mainly to a fall in the growth rate in agriculture and a deceleration in the growth of industry. Agriculture production in 1997-98 is likely to be lower than last year's record output. The foodgrains production in 1997-98 is expected to be 194.1 million tonnes compared with 199.3 million tonnes during 1996-97.

The growth of industrial production during 1997-98 is about 4.2 per cent. This is composed of a growth rate of about 4.9 per cent in mining, 3.6 per cent in manufacturing and 6.8 per cent in electricity. The slow growth of industry in 1997-98 followed growth of 7.1 per cent in 1996-97, which ,vas much lower than the 12.1 per cent growth achieved in 1995-96. The decline in investment seems to be an important factor in continuing industrial slowdown in 1997-98.

The annual rate of inflation, which was 6.7 per cent

at the start of 1997-98, had fallen to an eleven year low of 3.4 per cent by the end of August 1997. The low inflation rate of less than 4 per cent was maintained upto end of November 1997. Thereafter, there was a slight upward drift in the growth rate to over 5 per cent in December 1997 and close to 6 per cent in January 1998. The average inflation for 1997-98 was expected to be 1.4 percentage points less than the average inflation in 1996-97.

The foreign currency assets of RBI increased by US $ 5.3 billion in 1996-97 and by US $ 3.6 billion in 1997-98 to attain US $ 26.0 billion approximately at the end of March 1998. During, 1997-98, export growth slowed down significantly because of international and domestic factors. Import growth also decelerated on account -of continued industrial slackness.

All these developments in the economy have led to increasing demands on the infrastructure sectors, including communications. With expected acceleration in growth of agriculture, industry, trade and commerce, these demands are bound to grow and the infrastructure services have to keep pace with these developments.

Challenges and strategies

Postal administrations the world over are grappling with the challenges posed by growing volume of mail, the need to deliver services faster to the customers, increasing competition from courier industry and fast-changing communication scenario due to technological advancements. Worldwide and without taking account of regional particularities, economic factors are the prime movers determining the volume of letter-post traffic. Next come the postal factors i.e., the factors such as quality of service and infrastructure, which the postal administrations can influence. Social and demographic factors come third. A UPU study has shown that reduced in terms of percentage the increase or decline in traffic volumes with reference to each of these factors is as under:

– Economic factors	45%
– Postal factors	24%
– Social factors	21%
– Technological factors	10%

Postal administrations, under the aegis of the Universal Postal Union (UPU), are evolving strategies to respond to these challenges.

While universal and relatively cheap and affordable, postal service has to be provided to the society at large, the Post has also to cater to the specific needs of segments like the business and industry, government and institutional bodies who demand a much quicker service even at relatively higher cost. There is need for segmentation and prioritisation in the processing of different categories of mail like household mails, government mails, corporate sector mails, newspapers and magazines, other second-class mail which have different time-sensitivity. Modernisation of postal operations and induction of technology are important steps initiated by postal administrations to meet the challenges and improve services in order to enhance customer satisfaction.

Objectives of the department

The major objectives of India Post are to:

- ensure availability of basic postal services in all parts of the country, including tribal, hilly and remote areas;
- provide efficient, reliable and economic service;
- provide value-added services according to market requirements;

- modernize the services to handle the growing volume of work with efficiency and enhance customer and employee satisfaction;
- be a forward-looking organisation; and
- generate more resources and improve financial performance.

The Department has always endeavoured to provide basic postal services to the people at affordable price, and thus the basic postal services continue to enjoy considerable subsidy. Taking note of the changing customer needs, the 'Department of Posts has taken initiatives to introduce value added postal services at market competitive prices to Business and Industry. Establishment of Business Development Directorate in the Department is one step in this direction (refer Chapter 4). Introduction of Hybrid Mail Service using VSAT network is also in pursuance of this policy of enhancing customer satisfaction through more efficient and relevant services at a reasonable price.

Financial position

For the year 1997-98, it is estimated that out of 24 services, only 4 services are able to recover full cost and leave some profit margin on them for the Department. On the other hand, 20 services are subsidised, their cost of operation being more than the revenue realised. The total revenue during 1997-98 was Rs. 1566.52 crores against net working expenses of Rs. 2559.95 crores and the gap of Rs. 993.43 crores was managed through subvention.

Tariff

During 1997-98, postal tariff continued to be low and subsidised. 'Me subsidy ranges from 7% in respect of Parcel to 94% in respect of Registered Newspaper (Single). The Department subsidised Rs. 3.90 on

Registered Newspaper (Single) and Rs. 2.96 on Postcard to mention only a few services.

Postal operations

The Department is taking various steps to improve mail and delivery services in both urban and rural areas. Front Office operations of Post Office are being increasingly computerised. Computerisation of Mail Offices are also making strides.

The Department is sparing no efforts to make the management more responsive to public needs and expectations, make the services more customer friendly and humanise the system more perceptibly even as it inducts and assimilates increasing doses of technology into the operations to make the Post a better instrument of public utility and social integration.

2

Organisation

The Department of Posts under the Ministry of Communications continues to function under Shri Jagmohan, Minister for Communications. Shri Kabindra Purkayastha is Minister of State. Shri R.U.S. Prasad is the Secretary, Department of Posts, Director General, India Post and the Chairman of the Postal Services Board.

The Postal Services Board, the apex management body of the Department, comprises the Chairman and three Members. The three members of the Board hold portfolios of Operations, Development and, Personnel. The Joint Secretary and Financial Advisor to the Department is a permanent invitee to the Board. The Board is assisted by a senior staff officer of the Directorate as Secretary to the Board. Presently, Senior DDG (CP) is assisting the Board in this capacity. Dy. Directors General, Directors and Assistant Directors General provided necessary support for the Board at the Headquarters.

For providing postal services, the whole country has been divided into 19 Postal Circles. Each Circle is co-terminus with a State except the North Eastern Circle which comprises six North Eastern States; Maharashtra Circle includes the State of Goa; West Bengal Circle includes the State of Sikkim and the Union Territory of Andaman and Nicobar Islands; Kerala Circle includes the

Union Territory of Lakshadweep and Punjab Circle includes the Union Territory of Chandigarh. Each of these Circles is headed by a Chief Postmaster General. Each Circle is divided into Regions comprising groups of field units, called Divisions (Postal/RMS Divisions). Each region is headed by a Postmaster General who is the Postal Manager of the area. In the Circles and Regions there are other functional units like Circle Stamp Depots, Postal Stores Depots and Mail Motor Service, etc.

Over and above these 19 Circles, there is another Postal Circle, called Base Circle, to cater to the postal communication needs of the Armed Forces. Base Circle is headed by Additional Director General, Army Postal Service. The officer cadre of the Army Postal Service comprises officers on deputation from the civil post. 75 per cent of the other ranks of the Army Postal Service are also drawn from the Department of Posts and the remaining personnel are recruited by the Army.

Indian Post Offices are categorised as Head, Sub and Branch Post Office. Branch Post Offices are Extra-Departmental Post Offices (EDBOs) located in rural India. The Sub Post Offices, excepting a few, are departmental offices located in both rural and urban areas. Head Post Offices are graded into five categories according to their work load and staff strength, the largest being the General Post Offices at Mumbai and Calcutta, followed by GPOs at Ahmedabad, Bangalore, Chennai, Delhi, Kanpur and Lucknow.

The organisational set up of the Department which remained unchanged for decades has been undergoing restructuring in recent times, as a response to the challenges faced by the Post in the communication market due to induction of technology. This restructuring is designed to tackle the transitional problems of change and are primarily on functional basis giving due importance to the coordinating role of the higher management. Steps have been taken to substitute the traditional pyramidial system with desk level system to support the decision makers. These reforms are being introduced to infuse the system with dynamism and strengths that are I needed to create a responsive, sensitive, efficient and vibrant management system. Establishment of a "Business Development Directorate" in February, 1996, with the aim to design, develop, monitor and market various value added premium products of India Post, is also one of the' results of this restructuring.

3

Postal Operations

Postal network

India has the largest number of post offices in the world. Not only is the postal network well spread out, the delivery of mails too compares favourably with other countries, since the mail is delivered at the doorstep. Ours being a large country both in terms of area and population, the need for extension of postal facilities to rural areas has been receiving increased attention. While the emphasis in the rural segment is to provide basic postal services and network to bring these areas at par with the mainstream of economic and social life in the country, the need of the urban segment is for more efficient responsive communication service to serve the purpose of more specific business/professional and social sectors, a requirement that has gained greater significance and urgency in the wake of the economic liberalisation in the country.

At the time of Independence, India had 23344 post offices in the country, which were largely confined to the urban sector and selected villages. The Indian postal network has now grown to 153454 post offices in 1997-98. On an average, a post office serves an area of 21.4 sq. kms. & population of 5502. During 1997-98, the first year of the 9th Five-Year Plan, 402 EDBOs and 52 DSOs were sanctioned throughout the country. A target for opening 598 EDBOs and 50 DSOs has been set for Annual Plan 1998-99.

To further strengthen the network, following activities have been undertaken under the Plan Scheme "Expansion Of Postal Network":

(a) Opening of Extra Department Branch Post Office (EDBOs) in villages, preferably Gram Panchayat Head Quarters villages, where no post office exists at present and where such a post office is justified on the basis of norms prescribed, subject to availability of targets and resources. There is also a special emphasis on hilly, tribal and inaccessible areas.

(b) Upgradation of EDBOs into Departmental Sub Post Office (DSO) wherever justified, with particular emphasis on newly developed areas of the cities, industrial townships, etc. on norm based justification and availability of targets and resources.

Postal services

Postal operations at the post office encompass the entire gamut of the following basic postal services:

(i) Sale of stamps and stationery,

(ii) Booking of registered articles,

(iii) Booking of insured articles,

(iv) Booking of value payable articles, and

(v) Remittance of money through money orders and postal orders.

Traditionally, these services were provided at manual counters. The counter operations are being computerised progressively to reduce the waiting time for the customers and provide a range of services from the same counter. Computerisation of the counter operations has also provided the added benefit of streamlining backroom operations to improve after sale service. At present, more than 55 lakh transactions per month are being carried out at the computerised counters*

3.6 In order to give better security to insured articles, mailers have been allowed to post their articles in shrink wrapping materials.

As a measure, showing consideration to the age of senior citizens, it has been decided that elderly people will be given priority in being served at PO counters.

An Expert Group 'was set up to review the IPO Rules so that the same are updated and made simpler. The Committee has submitted its report in January 1998 which is under consideration in the Department.

Keeping in view the demand from general public and the trading community, the limit for ordinary money orders and VP articles has been raised 'from Rs. 2,000/- to Rs. 5,0001-.

Mail operations

Mail processing, transmission and delivery are the core activities of the Department of Posts. The letters are collected from 5.62 lakh letter boxes in the country. These are processed by a network of 573 Railway Mail Service (RMS) Offlices, and conveyed by trains, airlines, road transport, all over the country.

Mail volume

The mail traffic during the 1997-98 compared to previous year, is as given in Table 1.

Table 1
Mail traffic (in crores)

	Year	*1996-97*	*1997-98*	*Increase/ Decrease*
1.	Registered Articles	30.13	29.75	(-) 1.26
2.	Unregistered Articles	1479.52	1545.18	(+)4.44
3.	Total (I + 2)	1509.65	1574.93	(+) 4.32

Compared to the previous year, the Money Order traffic and their respective values during 1997-98 are as given in Table 2.

Table 2

Money order traffic and value of money order transmitted

	Year	*1996-97*	*1997-98*	*Increase/ Decrease*
1.	Money Order traffic (Numbers ir. crores)	11.16	11.08	0.72
2.	Value of MOs transmitted (Rs. in crores)	4101.77	4465.38	8.86

Mail management

The Department has identified different segments of mail traffic and has designated specialised handling for each segment. The specialised channels like Metro Channel for mails between Metro Cities, Rajdhani Channel for mails between National Capital and State Capitals and vice versa, Green Channel for local mails, Business Channel for bulk mails and Patrika Channel for newspapers and periodicals have been established.

Special arrangements to meet the sudden surges in traffic during festival season like Diwali and New Year were devised. In major towns public were invited to post their letters directly into destination bags.

The Department has started Computerisation/ Modernisation of the mail transmission/processing and delivery. The following was the achievement in this regard so far:-

Table 3

Offices Modernised and Computerised

	Activity	*1995-96*	*1996-97*	*1997-98*
1.	Modernisation of Mad Offices	22	26	21

2.	Computerisation of Registration Sorting	4	10	14
3.	Computerisation of Transit Mail Offices	–	2	6
4.	Mail Net	–	–	7
5.	Computerisation of Registration Delivery Work	–	–	1
6.	Computerisation of Head Record Offices	–	–	1

Modernisation of Mail Offices aims at providing better equipment and atmosphere of work in the Mail Offices.

Computerisation of Registration Sorting aims at speedier handling of registered articles and better response in case of complaint enquiries.

The Transit Mail Offices, especially at the airports in big cities, are crucial stages in transmission of mail. 'As a pilot project, the Department took up computerisation of Airport TMO work at Delhi and Mumbai during 1996-97. During 1997-98, 6 more TMOs have been computerised. The overall plan is to establish a connectivity between these different stages, so that data about an article keyed in once does not have to be keyed in again.

Material management

Material Management Division of the Directorate is entrusted with the responsibility of procuring, monitoring & supplying of quality materials, forms and equipments required for the day to day functioning of the vast Postal Network, throughout the country. A large variety of materials of different types and sizes like postal bags, letter boxes, uniform item, paper and other infrastructural equipment is either procured and supplied directly by Material Management Division or through the agencies of Directorate General of Supply and Disposal. The feeding to post offices is done through

46 Postal Store Depots (PSDs) and 5 Regional Form Depots (RFDs). These Depots work under the administrative control of Heads of Postal Circles where they are located. Apart from these Depots, there is a Postal Printing Press at Bhubaneswar.

For providing better in-house facilities, machinery and equipment is supplied PSDs/RFDs, and for the purpose of up-gradation of technology; to ensure better efficiency, accuracy and inventory control, computerisation, and networking of 46 Postal Store Depots has been undertaken.

Mail Motor Service (MMS)

For ensuring reliable and speedy conveyance of mails within large cities, and major towns, the Department operates its own fleet of mail motor vehicles., To ensure effective control over field activities, Department also maintain and operate its own staff cars and inspection vehicles. The MMS organisation ensures the maintenance, operations~ and administrations in respect of mail motor vehicles as well as inspection vehicles and staff cars of the Department of Posts.

On March 31, 1998 the strength of departmental vehicles was 1584 vehicles (including operation fleet of 1106 MMS vehicles, 451 inspection vehicles and 27 staff cars)

17 of the MMS stations have full-fledged workshop facilities for undertaking major repairs and maintenance jobs.

During 1997-98, the MMS vehicles covered 2.34 crore kms for conveying mails which is 9 lakhs kms more than the previous year. Total expenditure of Rs. 32.92 crores was incurred on MMS in 1997-98.

Besides taking number of steps for optimum utilisation of MMS fleet, 8 new additional vehicles were purchased and 42 MMS vehicles were replaced to cope with the requirement of increasing volume of mails and area of operation.

During the year under report, 74 new vehicles (in replacement of 65 inspection vehicles, 8 staff cars and one new inspection vehicle) were also purchased and provided to Circle/Region/Divisional heads for effective control over the field units.

Philately

Philately continued to be an important activity giving an opportunity to the Department to associate with the commencement of several significant national and international events. During the period from 1.4.97 to 31.3.98, forty-eight (48) commemorative/ special postage stamps have been issued.

To commemorate the 50th anniversary of India's Independence, the Department of Posts issued a special commemorative stamp on "India's Struggle for Freedom - three INA Stalwarts" Shah Nawaz Khan, P.K. Sahgal, G.S. Dhillon. This stamp was made available on 15th August 1997 through all district headquarters in the country. Stamps were also issued on other freedom fighters who worked for the country's Independence.

Indepex 97 - World Philatelic Exhibition was organised at New Delhi during 15.12.97 to 22.12.97 as the Department's homage to 50th Anniversary of Independence. To herald the exhibition, sets of, stamps on India's cultural and geographical heritage and bio-diversity and on Post Office theme were released.

Items of postal stationery, i.e. postcard, envelope, registered envelope, inland letter card and aerogram issued from 15.8.97 carried the inscriptioin "50th anniversary of India's Independence" in English and Hindi. In addition, 10 lakh pieces each of the five items of postal stationery were printed with the multicolour logo of 50th anniversary and distributed all over the country.

Since 1947, the Department of Posts has issued a large number of postage stamps on the theme of freedom struggle and related subjects. These stamps were displayed in all philatelic bureaux and counters all over the country from 15th August 1997 for the benefit of the public, especially to inspire the young generation. These exhibits were also displayed in Russia, Berne & Mexico.

To commemorate the 50th anniversary of Mahatma Gandhi's martyrdom, the Department issued a set of four stamps, with one design. Other highlights of the calendar of issues of commemorative/special stamps were the stamps on Birbal Sahni Institute of Palaeobotany, Lucknow in September 1997, Indian Medicinal Plants in October 1997 and 50th Anniversary of Declaration of Human Rights in March 1998.

Philately sale is carried out all over the country through 52 Philatelic Bureaux and 199 Philatelic Counters.

The following Circle/State Level Exhibitions -were held during the period :

(i) ORIPEX '97 Cuttack 27.6.97 to 29.6.97
(ii) MAPEX '97 Indore 22.8.97 to 24.8.97

4

Business Development Activities

Business Development Directorate was set up on 1.2.06 to design, monitor, develop and market value-added premium products of the Department of Posts. This Directorate completed its first anniversary on 1.2.97. The main responsibility of the Business Development Directorate is to ensure focused management of value added services. The Directorate is responsible for :

- The administration, expansion and promotion of the existing value added service;
- Planning and introduction of new value added products and services;
- Evolution procedures, regulations and guidelines for their retailing and networking;
- Market study, market testing and product improvement;
- Evolving market strategies, alliances and cooperation;
- Organising and sponsoring business training for personnel;
- Monitoring and review of growth of value added products and services;
- Exploring the scope of commercial utilisation of idle resources of the Department.

The Business Development Directorate is responsible for the marketing of the following customised value added products

(a) Speed Post

(b) Business Post

(c.) Corporate publicity

(d) Satellite Post

(e) Express Post

Marketing strategy

Business Development Directorate has designed during the last two years marketing strategies to retain household segments of business and to focus on corporate segments. A customised marketing strategy was adopted to position the various products, so that the corporate houses who comprise a very large proportion of clientele, are motivated to use speed post, Business Post and Corporate Publicity, as it is on them that these products are primarily targeted.

With this end in view, the Business Development Directorate arranged two separate workshops, one for the Directors of Postal Services (Additional GMs) of the metro cities and the other for the Circles who give us the remaining business. The Directorate also organised seminars, on premium products for managerial-level personnel. These seminars were held at the Postal Staff College, India.

The marketing strategy adopted basically was to reach out to the customer (a) through the direct marketing method and (b) through the conventional means.

The direct marketing method meant the following.

– Customers' meet is held in very circle with regular periodicity by the Head of the Circle/

Head of the Region, as an interface with prospective and existing customers.

- Direct mail is sent out from the Directorate as well as from the Head of the Circle, to likely customers.
- Tele marketing is done by marketing executives at the field level to canvass business.
- 'Personal visits are paid to the premises of potential and existing customers by marketing executives.

To generate awareness as well as a recall of its products, through the electronic as well as print media in a sustained manner, Business Development Directorate had campaigns on Doordarshan as well as in the print media.

Product development

The national network of Speed Post now extends to 78 stations with opening of three new stations at Ajmer, Rajkot and Hubli during 1997-98. Speed Post also provided a customised solution to various organisation. The revenue increased in speed post from Rs. 69.95 crores in 1996-97 to Rs. 77.95 crores in 1997-98.

To enable the corporate customers to outsource their pre-mailing operations, a new product called Mass Mailing (Business Post) was introduced from 1.1.97 in the cities of Delhi, Mumbai, Calcutta, Chennai, Hyderabad, Bangalore, Ahmedabad and Pune. This product takes care of insertion, enveloping, franking and addressing of articles to be posted/ hooked. To enable those customers who want to outsource only one or more activity, separate tariffs for collection, Insertion, Franking, Gumming and special handling have been prescribed.

Cornputerisation of speed post operations

To reduce and systematise operations at, the Speed Post Booking and Delivery Offices as, well as the Speed Post

Concentration Centres, a Track and Trace System was installed in 8 Metro Centres and 60 important Booking and Delivery Offices were brought under this system.

Computerisation has rationalised and simplified the process relating to storage of work papers, handling of complaints/claim and after sales services of Speed Post articles.

Mechanisation of delivery

To rationalise and customise delivery arrangement for Speed Post articles and other premium products delivery network was recognised and delivery through nodal offices has been arranged in most metro centres.

To effectively operationalise nodal delivery concept 90 mopeds have been supplied to some of the circles.

Rationalisation of speed post tariff

To provide a concessional rate for the article weighing upto 50 gms and meant for station within 200 km., a separate distance/weight slab was reintroduced and a revised tariff for such articles was prescribed w.e.f. 1.7.97. The tariff of these articles after this revision would cost a customer Rs. 20/-.

Revenue growth

A 'Comparative analysis of revenue generated in 1997-98 is as given in Table 4.

Table 4
Product-wise revenue growth of business development activities

Product 1996-97	*Revenue in 1997-98*	*Revenue in Increase*	*% of*
Speed Post	69.95 crores	77.95 crores	11.44%
Business Post	3.57 crores	20.21 crores	466.11%

Corp. Publicity	3.50 crores	4.27 crores	22.00%
Express Post	34.51 lakhs	66.75 lakhs	93.42%
Satellite Post	3.40 lakhs	5.04 lakhs	48.23%
Total	77.40 crores	103.15 crores	33.27%

5

International Relations

India has an important place in the fraternity of the postal administrations of the world. India is one of the earliest members of the Universal Postal Union (UPU), established in 1874. In 1948, the UPU became a specialised agency of the United Nations for assisting its 189 member countries in improving and developing their postal services. The Universal Postal Congress, is composed of representatives of all member countries. It meets every five years to lay down policy guidelines for postal legislation and development strategies. In order to make the union more flexible and responsive to the changes in the postal services, the 21st Universal Congress, held in Seoul in 1994, created two new elective Councils, the Council of Administration (CA) and the Postal Operations Council (POC). The POC is responsible for operational, commercial, technical and economic matters concerning the postal service, through its 9 committees.

India's contribution to the UPU found recognition in its election to both the Councils at the Seoul Congress. India also became the Chairman of the Finance Committee of the Council of Administration. The finance committee is responsible for consideration and approval of the Union Budget and financing the priority activities of the Union. India is also ex-officio member of the remaining five committees of the CA and the nine

Committees of the POC and has also been nominated to various working parties formed under these committees.

India played an active role in the Annual Session of Postal Operations Council which was held during 21st April to 2nd May 1997 and also in the Annual Session of Council of Administration held during 15th October to 24th October 1997. The Annual Sessions were held at Berne, Switzerland.

India attended the Government Board meeting of the Asian Pacific Postal Training Centre (APPTC) and the Executive Council (EC) meeting of the Asian Pacific Postal Union (APPU) held at Ho Chi Minh City (Vietnam) from 22nd September to 29th September, 1997. Matters relating to various aspects of the development of postal services in the region were discussed.

India also plays a meaningful role in the affairs of the Asian Pacific Postal Union (APPU), a Union of 26 countries of the Asian and the Pacific region. With a view to improve relations with its immediate neighbours, India also takes active interest in the Technical Committee on Communication$ (TCC) of the South Asian Association for the Regional Cooperation (SAARC). The SAARC, which comprises of 7 countries including India, was set up for regional cooperation in the South Asian Region. The 5th meeting of the SAARC Technical Committee on Communications (TCC) was held at Islamabad. India participated in the meeting held on 11th and 12th April 1997, where issues regarding promotion and cooperation in the field of Posts and Telecommunications; in the region were discussed.

An agreement on co-operation in the fields of Posts and Telecommunications between India & Belarus was signed at New Delhi in September 1997. A MOU on postal co-operation between the Postal Administration of

India and France was prepared and signed at Paris in January 1998. -

A training programme entitled !"Executive Development Programme" was organised at the Postal Staff College of India, Ghaziabad, for two weeks in March 1998 under the scheme of assistance in kind to the Universal Postal Union (UPU). Fellowships were granted by India to various overseas participants from the least developed countries viz. Bhutan, Mozambique, Nepal, Tanzania and Zambia. A Workshop on "Postal Business Development" was also organised at the Postal Staff College of India, in March 1998 under the SAARC Technical Cooperations Committee Calendar of Activities for the year 1997-98.

A number of important dignitaries visited India during 1997-98. The visitors included —

(i) Mr. Thomas E. Leavey, Director General, International Bureau of Universal Postal Union, Berne.

(ii) Mr. B. Boutenko, First Vice-Minister of Communications, Russia and also Chairman of the Postal Operations Council of UPU.

(iii) Ms. Joan Coulter, Director, Asian Pacific Postal Training Centre (APPTC), Bangkok (Thailand).

(iv) Mr. K.T. Fisher, Director, International Royal Mail, Great Britain.

(v) Mr. P.A. Qureshi, Regional Adviser of the Universal Postal Union, Jakarta (Indonesia).

(vi) Mr. Meghraj Gurung, Managing Director and Director General of Bhutan Post; and

(vii) Mr. Gem Tshering, General Manager (Operations) of Bhutan Post.

International mail service

International EMS

International EMS was introduced for nine more countries during the year 1997-98. These countries are Mongolia, Nepal, Botswana, Cayman Island, Namibia, Poland and Tanzania. With this, the International EMS Network now extends to 89 countries.

Surface Air Lifted (SAL) Mail Service for parcels was extended to seven more countries during this period with effect from 15.10.97. The seven countries are Egypt, Malaysia, Mauritius, Netherlands, Saudi Arabia, Seychelles and U.A.E. With this the SAL network now extends to 12 countries. The SAL service expedites the surface mails because in this service the mails are given air transmission between the countries.

One way International Business Reply Service (IBRS) commenced during the year. The purpose of the IBRS is to enable authorised senders to prepay in advance reply items posted by their respondents residing abroad. The service is meant basically for business houses. IBRS makes it easy for the companies overseas and customers/correspondents to respond to their mailings at no cost to them.

The 15th SAARC Letter Writing Competition was conducted on 10.8.1997. A total of 670 participants took part in this competition. The 27th UPU Letter Writing Competition was also conducted on 15.1.1998 in which 2777 students participated. The purpose of the Letter Writing Competitions conducted by UPU and SAARC Secretariat for Young People is to develop their faculty in composition and the subtley of their thought and to contribute to the strengthening of international friendship.

The traffic figures of both foreign Surface Parcels and Air Parcel Traffic are as under :

Table 5
Foreign surface parcel traffic

Year	Inward	Outward
1994-95	142244	56356
1995-96	89404	47433
1996-97	85823	49821
1997-98	58043	45341

Table 6
Foreign air parcel taffic

Year	Inward	Outward
1994-95	111506	657734
1995-96	140887	62770
1996-97	139827	45929
1997-98	107200	35859

Table 7
LC/AO mails - in Lakhs Kg.

Year	Inward	Outward
1994-95	39.72	22.81
1995-96	35.69	24.67
1996-97	38.98	23.68
1997-98	37.56	25.35

During the year 1997-98, the number of inward and outward Air Parcels were 1,07,200 and 35,859 respectively. During the same period, the number of inward surface parcels were 58,043 and the outward surface parcels were 45,341. There is a declining trend noticeable in the foreign parcel segment. This is a world-wide experience of postal administrations.

On the other hand, the outward LC/AO traffic has shown an increase of 7% in the year 1997-98 over the total outward traffic of 1996-97. Similarly, there has been increase in International Speed Post EMS in both outward and inward traffic. There was an increase of 3.96% over the previous year's traffic in Inward International Speed Post traffic and 15.68% increase in outward traffic in the 1997 compared to 1996.

Table 8
International speed post - EMS

Year	*Inward*	*Outward*
1995	318950	375282
1996	290868	331528
19977	301408	383537

Table 9
Foreign money orders (1997-98)

	Nos.	*Value (Rs. 000)*
Inward	60993	207992
Outward	8373	6038

During the year 1997-98, foreign money orders of the value of Rs. 20.79 crores were received as compared to Rs. 20.20 crores received in the 1996-97. The outward foreign money order for Nepal and Bhutan were to the value of Rs. 60.38 lakhs.

The Department received Rs. 28.76 crores on account of terminal dues, transit charges, etc. on international mail operations compared to Rs. 53.57 crores received in the year 1996-97 and Rs. 32.86 crores in the year 1995-96.

6

Modernisation

India Post has been in the process of computerising and automating postal operations since the early nineties. It is now having a close look at the following trends:—

(a) Post and mails is no longer a sector. It is a market—a communications market—there are alternative providers and deregulations are growing;

(b) Alternative means of communication pose a serious threat to the universal postal services, particularly driven by information technology;

(c) Customer needs are changing towards a demand for much greater speed, accuracy and reliability.

A Standing Committee on Technology was constituted in the Department consisting of representatives from the Indian Institute of Technology (IITs), the National Informatics Centre (NIC) and Department of Electronics, to aid and advice the Department in identifying appropriate and new technologies for existing services as also for new products and services, value additions and interfacing with other Government Departments, in the field of Information Technology. This Committee met twice during the year and provided valuable suggestions for effective induction of emerging technologies.

Counter operations

Hardware

India Post has recognised the need to keep pace with emerging technologies and processes for effective counter operations. A total of 918 Multipurpose Counter Machines (MPCMs), including those for savings bank LANs, were installed during the year 1997-98. The total number of offices having such machines went up to 1057 during the year under review. The number of transactions being conducted on these machines was of the order of 55 lakhs per month. Another 800 MPCMs are being installed during the year 1998-99. The Ministry of Personnel, Planning and Public Grievances has observed that MPCMs are an outstanding example of excellence in public services.

Software

During, 1.997-98, a policy decision was taken to standardise operating environment and application software in order to achieve inter-operability, connectivity and single point data entry, for access throughout the system, as quickly as possible. Windows NT/95/98 was accordingly selected as the operating environment.

A new savings bank software on Windows NT, Sanchay Post has been prepared, which takes care of all types of transactions pertaining to SB, RD, TD, National Savings certificates, IVPs, KVPs etc. The software has been extensively tested at the Postal Training Centre, Mysore, and has already been installed at 10 test sites. This software is under process of being installed at 170 other sites. During the year 1998-99 it is planned to be installed at 115 more sites~ This would enable a customer to carry out all kinds of transactions relating to all Savings Bank Schemes at the same counter.

The Postal Training Centre, Mysore, has taken up an ambitious task of developing an integrated software which takes care of all post office operations, excluding savings bank. This software. Meghdoot 98 is in an advanced stage of development and is expected to be installed in all major post offices in India by April, 1999. A truly world-class software, Mcghdoot 98 has been developed on Windows NT which aims at the total integration of front office with back office operations in a post office. This software is being validated by Indian Institute of Technology Kharagpur. This would enable computerisation of all post office operations. This would improve the speed and accuracy of all operations, including transactions with the customers.

Satellite money order service

During the year 1997-98, the existing network was further extended as a result of installation of 610 Extended Satellite Money Order Stations. The number of transactions being handled on the VSATs has gone up from a few thousands at its inception to over 7.5 lakhs per month. The resultant cost-benefit analysis has shown encouraging signs in terms of economics, particularly, resource inputs. Encouraged by the success of the technology, the Department has undertaken upgradation of some of the existing VSATs during the year 1998-99.

Hybrid mail service and corporate money order service

Installation of VSATs has enabled the Department to introduce two new value added products called Hybrid Mail Service (HMS) and Corporate Money Order Services. The former provides the facility to transmit text and data electronically from one VSAT to another to effect delivery of the same through the Postman as a postal article.

Installation of VSATs has also enabled the Department to send Corporate Money Orders upto Rs.

100 lakhs through VSAT to cater to the needs of the Corporate clients.

Automatic Integrated Mail Processing System (AIMPS)

After successful installation of AIMPS at Mumbai, Chennai and one advance coding suite at Anna Road Sorting Office, Chennai, the Department of Posts procured 9 stand-alone Coding Desks for installation at Mumbai in 4 Post Offices. The automatic integrated mail processing systems at Mumbai and Chennai are handling over 10 lakhs articles every day' This has enabled large volumes of mail to be processed in a short time.

Electronic Franking Machines (EFMs)

'The Department has decided that henceforth, the Franking Machines to be installed in the Post Offices and to be procured by customers for postal use will be only of the electronic variety. Apart from being versatile, the electronic franking machines have not only additional security features which make them tamper-proof and plug leakage of revenue, but are also amenable to remote access through the integration of information technology. 150 more EFMs are to be installed by 31st March, 1999.

Y2K

The advent of the new millenium, particularly the year 2000, is expected to pose a serious problem in computers which are not capable of recognising centuries and leap years in the embedded time and date clocks. Most operations in general, and the Savings Bank and Postal Life Insurance area, in particular, are critical to the Y2K problem. The Hardware and Software areas that are vulnerable to the bug have already been largely identified and effective steps are being taken to mitigate the impact of the problem within the expected time frame. A software has already been circulated to all Heads of Circles to identify non-compliant hardware. All new machines and software are being tested for Y2K compliance before procurement. This compliance is also being insisted for peripheral devices that will interface with Computers in the new millenium.

Web presence

The Internet's Worldwide Web is fast emerging as an affordable and globally accessible tool for information, communication and marketing. Through this network of networks, individuals and organisations are constantly in touch with each other and updating the knowledge base in the latest realms, besides aiding interaction between like-minded User Groups and individuals.

Recognising the potential of this tool for e-business and e-mail, the Department is setting up a Website at indiapost.org, which I will facilitate flow of information globally directed at potential users of postal services, connectivity to other postal administration, including UPU, and develop into a marketing tool for 'exportable' products, services and technologies.

During the 9th Five-year Plan, India Post will be sending 65% of its planned budget on induction of technology with a view to improving and upgrading the quality of service, meeting the emerging need of the customers and developing and providing new value added services and products. 'India Post will continue to take a close look at the technology options so that the postal products and services can be reoriented to the needs of the customers.

7

Agency Functions

Saving bank

Apart from providing basic postal facilities, the postal network, specially in rural India, has played a key role in encouraging the growth of small savings. The Post Office Savings Bank operates- through the wide network of post offices. The Department of Posts manages the work of Post Office Saving Schemes on behalf of the Ministry of Finance.

The following schemes are offered by the Department on behalf of Ministry of Finance

- Saving Account Scheme
- Recurring Deposit Scheme
- Time Deposit Scheme : I Year, 2 Years, 3. Years and 5 Years
- Monthly Income Scheme
- Public Provident Fund Scheme
- Indira Vikas Patra Scheme
- Kisan Vikas Patra Scheme
- National Savings Certificate
- National Savings Schemes, 1992.

Table 10

Saving schems : Business profile (as on 31.3.98)

Name of Saving Scheme	*No. of Accounts Rupees)*	*Total Amount (in lakhs of*
Saving Account (SB)	5,79,64,932	7,66,664
R.D. Accounts	3,83,99,036	9,26,151
T.D. Accounts	16,76,320	3,83,927
MIS Accounts	47,40,248	13,90,298
NSS 1992	5,84,724	87,875
PPF	9,24,341	2,41,599

Postal life insurance

Postal Life Insurance (PLI), introduced in 1884, is one of the oldest welfare scheme for the Government employees. The scheme was initially meant only for the postal employees. Today it caters not only employees of the Central and the State Governments, but also to Armed Forces personnel, employees of the local bodies, government aided educational institutions, universities, nationalised banks, many autonomous and financial institutions of the Government of India and Central and State Public Undertakings. In a major innovation, Rural Postal Life Insurance Scheme was introduced in 1995 for the benefit of people living in the rural areas.

For the financial year 1997-98, total business of 23,25,690 policies for the sum assured of Rs. 7065.37 crores was procured for PLI. This is against 22,54,897 new policies under written for a sum assured of Rs. 6215.81 crores in the previous year (1996-97).

PLI schemes were extended to rural areas, on 24.03.95. The business generated so far has been given in Table 11.

Table 11

Bunsiness generated in PLI schemes

Year	*Policies (in crores of' Rupees)*	*Sum assured*
1995-96	2,32,494	611.05
1996-97	1,66,019	458.77
1997-98	1,17,766	362.20

PLI and Rural PLI offer the following types of policies :-

- Whole Life Assurance
- Endowment Assurance
- Anticipated Endowment Assurance of 15 years and 20 years
- Convertible whole Life Assurance
- Yugal Suraksha

"Yugal Suraksha" is a new scheme under Postal Life Insurance, introduced with effect from 1.8.97. Yugal Suraksha provides insurance covet to the insurant and his/her spouse on payment of a single premium. Under this scheme, policy can be taken for a maximum sum assured of Rs. 3 lakhs by those who are between 21 and 45 years of age. The sum assured alongwith accrued bonus is payable to nominee/legal heir at the end of' the term.

A special plan entitled -10 year RPLI Plan" has been designed specially For persons living in rural areas. Its highlights are

(i) In case of' natural, calamities; the insurant need not pay the due premia for one year;

(ii) After one year the arrears of premia can be paid without interest; and

(iii) The policy does not lapse for one year in case of non-payment of due premia.

8

Finance

The net working expenses of the year was Rs. 2559.95 crore against the previous year's expenditure of Rs. 1917.88 crore (i.e. an increase of about 33 %). The increase was mainly due to implementation of 5th Pay Commission's recommendations.

From the year 1996-97 onwards the Department has been able to keep the working expenses within the ceilings approved by Ministry of Finance through strict budgetary control and close monitoring.

Table 1

Revenue and Expenditure (For the year 1997-98)

(Rs. in crore)

Particulars	*1996-97*	*1997-98*	*%age increase (+)/ decrease(-) over previous year*
1	2	3	4
Revenue			
Sale of Stamps	657.02	872.78	33%
Postage realised in Cash	297.80	407.32	37%

(Contd. . .)

1	2	3	4
Commission on Money Orders & Postal Orders	189.33	204.32	8% Indian etc.
Other Receipts	70.47	82.10	17%
TOTAL	1214.62	1566.52	29%
Expenditure			
General Administration	165.57	225.79	36%
Operation	2035.18	2462.47	21%
Agency Services	118.18	149.32	26%
Others	663.28	760.34	15%
TOTAL GROSS EXPENDITURE	2982.32	3597.92	21%
Less: Recoveries	1064.44	1037.97	2%
NET EXPENDITURE	1917.88	2559.95	33%

The level of earnings of the Department is in the form of 'Recoveries' and 'Revenue' on year to year basis. The item 'Recoveries' mentioned in Table 1 above represents the amount of commission earned by the Department for Agency Functions done on behalf of other Departments and organisations and the 'Revenue' is on account of sale of postal articles, commission on money orders and Indian Postal Orders and receipts from other premium services. These have been on the lower side in comparison to the working expenses incurred. This has resulted in a gradual increase in deficit and corresponding budgetary support from Ministry of Finance. The trend of increasing deficit every year can be arrested by controlling working expenses and also by increasing the earnings of the Department. However, substantial reduction in working expenses is not practicable as nearly 89% working expenses relating to salary, pension etc. are in the form of committed liability and thus not controllable. Improvement can be brought about only in the 'Revenue' receipts by adequatel increasing, tariff rates of postal articles, remuneration on account of agency functions and also by encouraging profit earning premium services such as Speed Post, Express Parcel Service, Hybrid Mail Service, Mass Mailing, Corporate Money Orders, etc.

Table 2

Recovery of working expenses on account of agency services in 1997-98

(Rs. in crore)

Sl. No.	Head of Account	1996-97	1997-98
1.	Saving Bank & Saving Certificate	907.01	969.67
2.	Military Pension	0.28	0.36
3.	Payment of Coal Miner and EPF/Family Pension & Misc. Services	9.78	1.98
4.	Payment of Railway Pension	11.22	6.00
5.	Postal Life Insurance	23.37	38.50
6.	Custom Duty realisation	0.82	0.79
7.	Saving Bank pairing work	0.73	0.00
8.	Mahila Samridhi Yojana	56.79	3.30
9.	Telegraph Share of combined offices	50.74	14.52
10.	Others	3.70	2.85
	Total	1064.44	1037.97

The funds made available by the Ministry of Finance for 'Working Expenses' and 'Capital Outlay, during the year were fully and appropriately utilised during the year. The surplus funds to the tune of Rs. 93.83 crores were surrendered in time to, the Ministry of Finance.

Fifth Pay Commission Report, the overall saving was only Rs. 8.69 crores which was very nominal. This appreciable achievement could be made possible by effective budgetary control and by monitoring progress of expenditure on month to month basis.

Table 3

Funds Surrendered and Savings During 1997-98

(Rs. in crores)

Nature of expenditure		*Budget Est. including Supplementary Grant*	*Actual Expenditure*	*Excess (+)/ Saving (–)*	*Amount Surrendered*	*Savings*
3201	Working Expenses (Voted)	3677.68	3597.92	79.76	73.70	6.06
5201	Capital Outlay	74.34	51.58	22.76	20.13	2.63
	Total	3752.02	3649.50	102.52	93.83	8.69

Capital outlay

The expenditure on fixed assets in the year 1997-98 was Rs. 53.76 crores. Of this, 35.84% was on land and buildings and 64.16% on apparatus, plants and others. The value of Capital on fixed assets rose to Rs. 827.95 crores at the end of the year. The net progressive fixed asset value upto the end of the year was Rs. 690.59 crores.

Cost of services

The cost and revenue of main services for the year 1997-98 alongwith the position for the previous year are as shown against each service below:—

Table 4
Cost of services (In Rs.)

Services	*1996-97 (Projection)*		*1997-98*	
	Cost	*Revenue*	*Cost*	*Revenue*
1. Post Card	2.20	0.15	2.72	0.25
2. Printed Post Card	1.99	0.80	2.52	1.42
3. Competition Post Card	–	–	2.72	2.00
4. Letter Card	2.27	0.75	2.84	0.96
5. Letter	2.63	2.12	3.14	3.22
6. Parcel	23.47	24.65	27.50	29.91
7. Money Order	18.13	17.80	24.26	15.82
8. Registration	13.68	7.00	16.87	9.67
9. Insurance book post	19.05	26.07	23.68	41.90
10. Book pattern and sample packets	3.52	2.04	4.88	2.70
11. Printed books	4.94	1.80	7.45	2.25
12. Others	4.95	1.46	6.43	2.08

9

Human Resource Development

The strength of an organisation is dependent on its people. The Department with a strength of 6,04,257 personnel has a well developed training infrastructure. Over the years, it has tried to follow a policy of human resource development in consonance with the emphasis on introduction of technology in postal operations. It has worked out an extensive training programme, both on the job as well as institutional, for upgradation of skills of the managers and operatives and enhance their professional knowledge.

Training infrastructure

The training infrastructure of the Department consists of the following Training Institutes :

(1) Postal Staff College of India, Ghaziabad; and

(2) Regional Postal Training Centres at Darbhanga, Madurai, Mysore, Saharanpur and Vadodara.

Postal staff college

9.3 The Postal Staff College of India at Ghaziabad is the apex training institution catering to the training needs of the managerial cadres of the Department. The primary objective of this college is to impart induction as well as inservice training to the officers of the Indian Postal Service and Postal Service Group 'B' with a view to:

– inculcate requisite knowledge, skills and attitude to enable them to make the Postal

System effective and responsive to customers' needs;

- undertake and promote research in spheres of management of the Postal Services; and
- build 'up a Postal Data Bank and Documentation Centres.

In addition, the college also organises workshops on different aspects of the Postal Services at the behest of the Universal Postal Union and under the agreement among SAARC countries for the benefit of officers belonging to Foreign Postal Administrations.

During the period under review the college conducted .6 Induction and 9 Inservice courses. In all 283 officers participated in these courses. Also during this period 212 officers have been imparted training in computers.

An Executive Development Programme was organised from 9.3.98 to 20.3.98 with participation of foreign officers from Mozambique, Tanzania, Zambia, Nepal and Bhutan, including officers from India.

A workshop on postal Business Development was organised under the programme of SAARC activities from 23rd March to 27th March 1998. Officers from Nepal, Maldives, Bangladesh, Pakistan and Sri Lanka attended the workshop, alongwith participants from India.

Indian Postal Service officers trained abroad are as under :

(1)	APPTCM, Bangkok	12
(2)	SIDA, Sweden	1
(3)	China	1
(4)	JICA, Japan	2

The following heads of foreign postal administrations and training institutions visited PSCI, Ghaziabad :

(i) Mr. H.E.M. Mimoun Aoujil, Secretary General of Ministry of Posts and Telecom, Morocco on 8.4.97.

(ii) Ms. Joan Coulter, Director, APPTC, Bangkok on 15.4.97.

(iii) Mr. Meghraj Gurung, DG, Bhutan Post on 28.1.98.

Regional postal training centres

The main objectives of the Regional Postal Training Centres are:

- To impart induction training to Inspectors (Postal) and (RMS) and Time-scale Postal and Sorting Assistants;
- To impart Inservice refresher training to Postal and Sorting Assistants, Supervisors, Inspectors, ASPOs, Postmasters, etc.; and
- To impart the skill and knowledge required to understand and operate computer hardware and software systems relevant to the needs of the Department.

A total number of 16,418 officials were imparted training during the period from 1st April, 1997 to 31st March 1998 by the five Regional Training Centres, A total of 3008 officials were imparted training in computers.

Recognition of higher performance

Meghdoot Awards were introduced in the -Department of Posts in 1984 to 'reward employees of the Department for excellence in service and selection for award is made by a Committee of senior officers in the Department from nominations sent by the various Circles. Up to the year 1997, the awards were given for ten categories covering

Extra Departmental agents and Departmental personnel from Group A and all ' categories of B, C and D. A new category (XI) was introduced in 1998 for officials who have done outstanding team work in furt ance of an activity sponsored by the Department.

Meghdoot Award carries a cash prize of Rs. 51,0001- and a scroll. In case of the category introduced in 1998 the cash award of Rs. 51,000/- is distributed equally among team members, and individual scrolls are Oven to each team member.

10

New Initiatives

Information technology

The Standing Committee on Technology under the Chairmanship of the Member (Operations) which also has representatives from the Departments of Electronics and Telecommunications as well National Informatics Centre and IIT Delhi has been constituted on the basis of a decision taken by the Postal Services Board. The Standing Committee is to determine new services and products and identify appropriate technologies. The Standing Committee has already had two meetings on 11.11.1998 and 30.11.1998.

Three projects were approved by the Postal Services Board as a part of continuous collaboration with the Indian Institutes of Technology. The Tracking and Tracing System is being studied by IIT, Delhi. The Electronic Point of Sale Project is being examined by IIT, Kharagpur in close collaboration with Postal Training Centre, Mysore and a project relating to devising of an electronic chip for recording details of movement of bags/articles, is being handled by IIT, Mumbai.

Postal Training Centre, Mysore is in the process of developing 'Meghdoot 98', a complete software for the Post Office in a LAN environment. They are trying to develop an integrated package for post office operations whereby the different branches can have an in built flexibility of drawing data specific to them and utilising the same according to their requirements. The software takes care of all counter transactions (excluding savings bank) and dispatches, pay bills, pensions and scheduled, BO summary, SO summary, HO summary, HO cash book, all treasury functions, registration delivery, money order payment. The software is being developed on client/ server architecture with GUI based application. It is being developed on Windows NT Platform and MS SQL server in accordance with the guidelines issued by the Directorate in this regard. The software is being evaluated and validated by IIT Kharagpur The software is being tested at Hyderabad GPO, Indore HO and Gwalior HO. This software would be in position in all major post offices in India by middle of 1999.

The Postal Machines Repair Organisation, created in 196 5-66 for maintenance/servicing of postal machines, has been overtaken by the changes that have occurred during the last five years as a result of induction of modem technology. The Postal Services Board in its meeting held on 14.8.98 has decided to re-organise the same. The entire work force including the Managers and the Dy. Managers as well as PMAs and supervisors are being imparted training at the Postal Training Centre, Mysore in new skills pertaining to handling of hardware. Orders are under issue for re-locating the existing personnel depending on the requirements of the various Circles.

An Expert Group was set up to determine the parameters for approval of franking machines for public use. The Expert Group which had representatives from the Department of Electronics and Indian Institute of Technology, Delhi determined the short and long term parameters. Franking machines are being approved at present with reference to these parameters.

A new generation of franking machines which uses codes for charging have recently come into the market necessitating a code management policy for the new generation of franking machines. A code management policy with the approval of the Postal Services Board has been determined and suitable instructions in this regard have been issued to the field formations on 18.7.1998.

Postal pperation

Renewed launching of Panchayat Sanchar Sewa Yojana (PSSY)

With the 73rd Amendment to the Constitution of India, Panchayats have become a third tier of the administration. It was, therefore, considered appropriate to enlist this active structure. The scheme through which this is done is, the Panchayat Sanchar Sewa Yojana (PSSY). The PSSY is a new tier added to the postal network where panchayats appoint a local youth having a minimum qualification of pass in the 10th standard, as an agent of the panchayat in the Panchayat Sanchar Sewa Kendras.

The scheme has a great potential to provide postal counter services to the rural areas in the country where we are not able to open a post office. The scheme was launched in 1905 as a pilot project in 5 States. Presently 613 PSSKs are functioning in the country. An intensive drive has been undertaken during the last six months to popularise the PSSY. The Heads of Postal Circles Raised with Chief Secretaries of the State Governments to enlist complete cooperation by the later. Simultaneously, an exercise was started to approach the Gram Panchayats without a post office to indicate their willingness to introduce the scheme in their village. A very significant progress in the matter of opening of PSSKs is expected in the near future.

Saving Bank

The report of the Expert Group on Remuneration to

Department of Posts for the Operation of Savings Bank in Post, in one of its recommendation had suggested that the Department of Posts, at the beginning of the each financial year, give a broad outline of computerisation schemes/projects of savings bank operation along, with the estimated cost, to Ministry of Finance. After acceptance by DEA it be implemented by them.

The issue was again taken up in the committee on Small Savings which was impressed upon the idea of funding of the computerisation projects of savings bank in post offices by Ministry 'of Finance as it is an agency function on behalf of Ministry of Finance only.

In its recommendation and also in principle MOF has now agreed that Rs. 30 crore be given to Department of Posts for Computerisation of savings bank operation of all HOs in the country.

Postal life insurance

The various policies being offered under PLI have been given appropriate trade names for improving their market ability. Accordingly, Suraksha is Trade name given to Whole Life Assurance, Suvidha to Convertible Whole Life, Santosh to Endowment Assurance and Sumangal to Anticipated Endowment Assurance. Similarly, in Rural PLI, the respective policies have Gram as suffix before the Trade names. The 10-year RPLI has Trade name of Gram Priya.

The items of work involved in after-sales servicing of PLI/RPLI have been taken up for computerisation. A software for preparation of Schedule by HOs on computers and transmitting the same through floppies has also been developed. This will enable posting by loading the information direct on the system in the Circle office. Similarly software for management information system (MIS) has also been developed which will help in monitoring, control and after sales service. The operative work in the office of DPLI. Calcutta is also being computerised.

Postal accounts

It was decided to transform the functioning of the Postal Accounts Offices into a modem one by latest and appropriate technology in order to ensure efficient, fast and accurate accounting of the Department of Posts during the 9th Plan Period in a phased manner. Accordingly, in the Annual Plan 1997-98, the work relating to monthly accounts compilation, G.P.F. & Pay bill in all the Postal Accounts Offices including .-Book Section of the Directorate was taken up for computerisation.

The process to amend the Indian post office act 1898

It was decided to undertake review of the Indian Post Office Act which is 100 years old. A committee was set up for carrying out a comprehensive reviews of the Act keeping in view the technological developments and also taking) into account the recommendations made in the technology action plan submitted by the Prime Minister's National Task force on Information Technology and Software Development, the Committee submitted its report incorporating recommendations for amendments to the Indian Post Office Act. 'Me report of the Committee is under examination.

Personnel

Career prospects

Consequent to the amendment of the Recruitment Rules for Indian Postal Service Group 'A' in 1997 providing for representation of promotee officers in the service upto 33-1/3% of the cadre strength and temporary down-gradation of STS posts to the extent of non-availability of regular STS officers, as many as 140 Postal Services Group '13' Officers were promoted to Group 'A' in July 1998.

Also 12 JAG officers were promoted to SAG in August 1998 and 2 SAG officers were promoted to Sr. DDG/CPMG grade in September 1998.

In keeping with the orders of the Apex Court on the subject of protection of women in work places and consequent orders of the Department of Personnel & Training detailed instructions have been issued for formation of prescribed committee at various levels in the Department.

11

Activities

Staff relations

The Department endeavoured to maintain healthy and purposeful relations with the three Federations and twenty seven Unions/Associations of Departmental employees and Extra-departmental Agents.

The re-verification process for purpose of recognition of services associations under the CCS (RSA) Rules 1993, was successfully conducted in the Department of Posts. As a result of this process, a total of 16 service associations, including one representing ED Agents under EDA (RA) Rules 1995, have been granted recognition for a period of two years. There was 80% participation of the employees in the re-verification process. The next phase of verification in respect of the service associations whose recognition lapses in April, 1998 has also been initiated.

During 1997-98, two Federations and 12 Associations were granted periodical cum Standing Committee Meetings. In addition, a special meeting with the representatives of recognised associations was held to review the issues -relating to the problems of overtime allowances in Post Offices.

Joint Action Committee of the Postal Associations had proposed to go on an indefinite strike w.e.f. 24.9.97, which however was later withdrawn after the implementation of the recommendations of the 5th Central Pay Commission. Another notice of indefinite strike from 18th November, 1997, was received from Postal and RMS employees, demanding immediate implementation of Talwar Committee recommendations and upgradation of Postmen's pay. This strike was deferred by the associations after a personal appeal issued by the Minister of Communications and detailed discussions the associations had with the Secretary, Department of Posts. Later, a one day Token Strike on 5.1.1998, was held by the associations, in support of their demands. The Department took all precautionary measures to minimize dislocation of mail service and disruption by the strikers on the day of strike. The strike called by the Accounts Officers and Accounts Employees Association of the Department of Posts, demanding upgradation of their pay scales, was also deferred after a meeting of the association with Secretary, Department of Posts.

Staff welfare

The objectives of the Postal Services Staff Welfare Board are to promote, develop, organise and exercise control in respect of staff amenities and welfare, sports and cultural activities in the Department. The Board receives grant-in-aid for this purpose from the Government funds. Voluntary contributions from the staff and collection through Sports and Cultural activities are also arranged by the subordinate formations.

The funds of the Welfare Board are utilised for activities like Sports, Recreation Clubs, financial assistance in cases of illness, death and natural calamities, educational scholarships, subsidy for excursion trips, grants to help handicapped staff and their children, vocational training centres and creches etc. During 1997-98, an amount of Rs. 225 lakhs was allotted for the welfare activities.

During 1997-98, Postal Services Staff Welfare Board decided to enhance the quantum of financial assistance to the victims of fire, floods and natural calamities to Rs. 15001- in case of departmental employees and Rs. 750/- for Extra-Departments Agents. The rates of scholarships for the wards of postal employees have also been enhanced. In addition, benefits available to Departmental and ED employees suffering from T.B. were also improved.

Holiday homes

11.8 The Department is running 18 Holiday Homes for the benefit of its employees and their families. These we quite popular and well made use of by the staff.

Sports

During 1997-98, All India Postal Services Tournament in Weightlifting, Powerlifting, Best Physique, Chess and Carrom, Volley Ball, Table Tennis, Kabaddi, Athletics and Cycling, Basketball, Wrestling. Cricket, Football and Hockey were organised. In I addition, All India Cultural Meet was held at Calcutta. A number of sports persons from the Department participated in National/ International Championships in various events. Allocation for sports activities was enhanced during the year.

Magazine

Dak Patrika is a quarterly magazine (House Journal) of the Department of Posts, published bilingually. This is the media of the Department of Posts to let its plans and schemes known to everybody in the Department through various articles written by the Departmental officials and Officers. Besides, the magazine is an effective platform for displaying the abundant talent of those working in the Department by publishing their articles, stories and poems etc. A special issue of the magazine on "Indepex" was brought out during 1997-98, which contained special articles on future of Postal Services, Gandhi Service Stamps and other interesting topics. The issue got compliments from a large number of Postal employees, officers and ~ general readers.

Medical facilities

The Department attaches great importance to provide medical facilities to its employees and their family members. The Department of Posts, alongwith Department of Telecommunications, runs 56 P&T Dispensaries and 7 first-aid Centres in 48 cities/towns. The number of beneficiaries served by these dispensaries is about 7.6 lakhs. 'Me expenditure incurred on the running of the Dispensaries, including the cost of medicines, during 1997-98 was Rs. 22.16 crores. In other cities and towns, Postal staff availed the services of CGHS dispensaries or Authorised Medical Attendants.

Compassionate appointments

In the event of the death of departmental officials and extra-departmental agents while in service, and in certain cases of invalidation of officials in service, the Department provides suitable appointment to a family member of the official concerned in relaxation of normal recruitment rules in deserving cases.

Representation of SC and ST service

As on 31.3.98, there are 19062 ST, 54359 SC, 2647 Ex-servicemen, 128 Disabled Ex-servicemen and 31027 Women employees in various grades in the Department (see Table No. 21 & 22).

Work study

The Work Study section carried out work studies of MV, SPG, Philately and Vigilance Sections of the Department. The work study reports in respect of SPG, MV and Philately Sections have been issued. The work study report in respect of Vigilance Section has been prepared. A study for creation of posts of Sr. Hindi Officer in the subordinate and attached offices has also been carried out. The IWSU has recommended ten additional posts of Sr. Hindi Officers.

A study for evolution of norms for Group "C" employees connected with payment of pension under the provision of Coal Mines Family Pension Scheme 1971 was completed and the report on same is under preparation.

A study for evolution of norms for the post of PRI Franking machines has been approved by SIU, Ministry of Finance. A study for evolution of norms for Rural PLI Bonds has been finalised. A study connected with EDAs Group Insurance Scheme has been completed.

The following studies are underway :

(1) To evolve norms for Group 'C' staff connected with MPCMs in the Post Offices;

(2) To evolve norms for Sub-Divisional IPOs/ ASPOs;

(3) To evolve norms of Group 'C' staff connected with savings bank work manually in Post Offices. The study was completed and given to SIU for vetting. The SIU did not agree to the norms suggested. The joint study will be undertaken on the dates convenient to, SIU; and

(4) To evolve norms for Supervisory staff connected with Speed Post in Delhi.

Official language

The Department of Posts, as per the policy of the Central Government, has been making sustained efforts to ensure the optimum use of Hindi as Official Language. To ensure the implementation of Official Languages Act, 1963, Official Language Implementation Committee has been constituted at the headquarters and also in all its subordinate offices.

With a view to ensure the maximum progressive use of Hindi as Official Language, a scheme of organising "RAJBHASHA SAMMELAN" in every circle of the Department, at least once in a year, has been introduced and notable progress has been made in this regard.

Three Rajbhasha Sammelans have been organised in Maharashtra, Orissa and West Bengal circles during the year 1997-98. Steps taken to ensure solutions to various difficulties faced by the Circles have been proved effective.

With a view to review the implementation of the Official Languages Act and rules made thereunder, the Official Language Policy and compliance of the Annual Programme issued by the Ministry of Home Affairs, Department of Official Language, inspection of various offices of the Department is being carried out from time to time and so far three subordinate offices were inspected at the Directorate level.

With a view to gear up the implementation of Official Language Policy through incentive and goodwill, a number of incentive schemes have been introduced in the Headquarters and subordinate offices. The officers/ staff are duly recognised with the cash prizes under these schemes.

The Department has introduced an "ALL INDIA DAK VIBHAG RAJBHASHA SHIELD SCHEME" for its subordinate offices. Under this scheme, three running shields and a cash prize of Rs. 5,0001- are awarded every year to three circles located in regions "A", "B" and "C" for doing the maximum work in Hindi.

Besides, second and third prizes of Rs. 4000/ - and 3000/- each, respectively are also awarded to the circles located in regions "A" and "C". The Department provides adequate funds every year to its circle offices and their subordinate offices for purchase of Hindi books for their libraries, as per the norms prescribed by the Department of Official Language.

Instructions have been issued regarding provision of training of officers and staff at the Headquarters and the Circles under various schemes initiated under Hindi Teaching Scheme.

"HINDI FORTNIGHT' was organised in the Directorate from 12th to 26th September 1997. Besides other officials, senior officers of the Directorate at the DDsG level took part in the fortnight with enthusiasm. Maximum work was done in Hindi during that period. The officers/staff were encouraged by awarding prizes. The prizes were distributed by the Secretary (Posts)

Inspection

The Inspection Organisation of the Directorate carried out inspection of 8 circle offices, Postal Staff College (1), Office of the Chief Engineer Civil, Bangalore and 4 Regional Offices during 1997-98 The DDG (1, QM & PG) had visited 20 field units of post offices and Mail Offices during the year.

Public grievances

During 1997-98, the Department handled 8,57,041 cases of public grievances out of which 7,76,775 cases were settled in the year itself. Thus the percentage of settlement of cases was 90%. As an ongoing procedure, Dak Adalats were continued to be held. Four Dak Adalats held during 1997-98 at Circle level, handled 1216 complaints.

Out of these, 1097 complaints were settled on the spot and detailed inquiries were initiated in the remaining cases. In order to rationalise the system of handling public grievances, 67 Computerised Customer Care Centres were set up at important places in different Circles during 1997-98.

These centres have been set up at Guwahati (Assam), Hyderabad, Vijayawada and Visakhapatnam (Andhra Pradesh), Delhi (Delhi), Ahmedabad, Rajkot, Surat and Vadodara (Gujarat), Bangalore, Dharwad and Mysore (Karnataka), Trivandrum and Cochin (Kerala), Mumbai, Pune and Solapur (Maharashtra), Bhopal, Indore and Jabalpur (Madhya Pradesh), Bhubaneshwar and Cuttack (Orissa), Chandigarh, Jalandhar Amritsar and Ludhiana (Punjab), Jaipur, Ajmer and Jodhpur (Rajasthan), Chennai, Arakkonam, Kancheepuram, Chegalpatti, Vellore, Karaikudi, Karur, Kumbakonam, Mayliadhutturai, Puttokotai, Padukottai, Srirangam, Thanjavur, Vrindhachallam, Trichy, RMS, Dindigul, Kanya Kumari, Kovil Putt, Periya Kalan, Ramanathapuram, Trinulveli, Tuticorin, Virudhunagar, Madurai, SSRM Madhurai, and C.C.C. Madurai, Tiruchirapalli, Coimbatore, Dharmapuri, Erode, Namakkal, Nilgiris, Pollachi, Salem, Tirupur, Sivaganga and Nagapattinam (Tamil Nadu) and Calcutta (West Bengal).

Postal buildings

During 1997-98, 275 Staff Quarters, 4 Administrative Offices and 54 other buildings were constructed. On the 50th Anniversary of India's Independence, important Heritage buildings were illuminated all over the country from 15th August 1997 to 30th August 1997, for which funds to the tune of Rs. 19.27 lakhs were spent.

Expansion of postal network

Against a target of opening of 598 Extra-departmental Branch Post Offices (EDBOs) and 50 Sub Post Offices (DSOs), subject to the availability of resources, during the year 1998-99, so far 24 EDBOs and 7 DSOs have been sanctioned throughout the country.

Modernisation

Activities relating to modernisation of mail processing proposed till 31.3.1999 are as given in Table 1.

Table 1
Modernisation of mail processing

	Activity	*Target*
1.	Modernisation of Mail Offices (No)	42
2.	Computerisation of Transit Mail Offices (No)	5
3.	Computerisation of Registration Sorting Centres (No)	7
4.	Upgradation of Operational Equipments for Delivery	160
5.	Modification of BG Full Postal Vans	24

Technology upgradation

The progress in this field has been as indicated in Table 2.

Table 2
Progress on technology upgradation

Activity	*Upto 31.3.1998*	*From 1.4.1998 to 31.12.1998*	*Anticipated from 1.1.1999 to 31.3.1999*
1. Multipurpose Counter Machines (MPCM)	3107	359	562
2. Savings Bank Local Area Network (SB LAN)	246	28	106
3. Micro Earth Stations for Satellite MO, (SMO)	75	0	0
4. Upgradation of Existing Earth Stations	0	0	21
5. Extended Satellite Money Order	700	0	0

6.	Automatic Integrated Mail Processing System (AIMPS)	2	0	0
7.	Electronic Franking Machines (Lower end)	290	0	150
8.	Stamps Cancelling Machines (SCM)	722	0	20

Corporate planning

National Postal Policy: A paper on National Postal Policy was prepared. The same has been submitted for approval of competent authority.

This policy paper has laid emphasis on upgradation and modernisation of postal services with enhanced application of modem technology, expansion of postal network through traditional methods of opening of post offices as well as through innovative methods like franchising at minimum cost, involvement of private initiative in postal services particularly in the areas of value added services, generation of additional resources, compliance with the principle of universal service obligation and strengthening international cooperation in the field of postal services on bilateral basis and through the aegis of Universal Postal Union and other regional postal bodies engaged in the task of postal development.

Citizen's Charter: With a view to informing the members of the public about the various services being provided by the Department as also to emphasise the Department's commitment to provide better quality of services and indicate where to go in the case of a grievance, a Citizen's Charter was prepared.

The draft Charter has been sent to the Ministry of Personnel for their comments. Approval of the competent authority would be obtained before finally notifying the Charter.

Business development

Business Development Directorate chalked out product-wise targets and Business Action Plan for all Circles during a Business Meet held in July 1998. A Marketing Management was conducted for Senior Officers in November 1998 and a Speed Post Workshop was conducted in October 1998 for Group A and Group B officers.

To streamline the delivery of Speed Post, nodal delivery system was implemented in all the metros. A dedicated delivery staff has been provided in all these nodal delivery offices to effect Speed Post delivery. As a Marketing Strategy, collection of Speed Post and other Premium Products has been outsourced in Mumbai and Delhi. The objective is to provide the convenience to retail and corporate customers as well as to increase business.

The Speed Post network now extends to 81 sections. Department has earned a revenue of Rs. 70 Crores from all Premium Products upto October 1998.

Postal life insurance

The target of new business in PLI and Rural PLI has been set at Rs. 880 crores and Rs. 500 crores respectively, for the year 1998-99. By the end of November 1998, business of Rs. 325.87 crores in 48159 PLI policies and Rs. 97.65 crores in 29513 Rural PLI policies has been secured. The targets are expected to be achieved by the end of March 1999.

RPLI operations have been computerised in 4 Regions of the Andhra Pradesh Circle- by the end of December, 1998. The same would be computerised by the end of March, 1999 in the remaining 27 Regions.

PLI operations in the Office of Director, PLI Calcutta are to be computerised by the end of March 1999 for which approval has been received.

Philately

During the period from 1.4.1998 to 30.11.1998, 34 commemorative/special stamps have been issued. The Department of Posts commemorated the 50th anniversary of India's Independence by releasing a number of stamps on freedom fighters. This was concluded with the issue of a special commemorative stamp on 15th August 1998. On this occasion, the stamp was made available at all district headquarters in the country.

A new definitive stamp in the denomination of 300 (P) carrying the message of Pulse Polio was released on 21.9.1998. Items of postal stationery, i.e. Inland letter card and SPC printed in multicolour and carrying the message of UDHR were released on 16.11.1998.

The Department has brought about more than 170 commemorative stamps during the last 50 years to remember and relieve the glorious moments in our freedom struggle. These stamps were displayed in all philatelic Bureau.

Philatelic sale is carried out all over the country through 53 Philatelic Bureau and 199 Philatelic Counters.

The following Circle/state level Exhibition was held during the reference period :

(i)	NEPEX-98	Shillong	23.4.98 to 25.4.98

During the remaining period of the year, following Circle/State level Exhibitions are planned:

(i)	GUJPEX-98	Vadodara	17.12.98 to 19.12.98
(ii)	MAHAPEX-98	Nashik	28.12.98 to 31.12.98

During 1.12.1998 to 31.3.1999, it is proposed to issue about 15 Commemorative/Special Stamps.

International relations

India, being a member the Postal Operations Council (POC) and the Council of Administrations (CA), the two organs of the Universal Postal Union (UPU), participated in the annual sessions of these Councils which were held from 21st April to 6th May 1998 and from 11th October to 22nd October 1998 respectively, at Berne, Switzerland. India attended the meetings of all the 9 Committees of the POC where matters on terminal Dues, Parcel Post, EMS, Quality of Service, Marketing, Seoul Postal Strategy were discussed. In the CA, India chaired the meetings of the Finance Committee and of the Working Party on "Financing Union Activities", besides attending the meetings of its other 5 Committees. India is also a member of the Strategic Planning Working Party and the Working Party on Languages and participated in these meetings also.

The Governing Board meeting of the Asian Pacific Postal training centre (GB-APPTC) and the executive council meeting of the Asian Pacific Postal Union (APPU) were held at Wellington (New Zealand) from 13th September to 18th September 1997. A two member delegation represented India in this meeting, where matters relating to various aspects of the development of postal services in the region like Business Plan, Budget, special Activities in the region, APPU Action Plan, Working of Asia Pacific Post and Regional Support Centre, were discussed.

The conference of Commonwealth Postal Administrations (CCPA) was held at Kuala Lumpur (Malaysia) from 24th to 28th September 1998. A two member delegation represented India in this meeting, where challenges facing the Post and how the Commonwealth Postal Administrations can respond to them were discussed.

Mr. Ibrahim Rashad, Managing Director and Mr. Hussain Hameed from Maldives visited India to study the Indian Postal System in November 1998.

India would attend the Joint Annual Session of the Postal Operations Council and the Council of Administrations scheduled to be held in February 1999 at Berne, Switzerland.

International mails

International Speed Post Network was extended to 8 more countries during the year 1998. With effect from 1st August 1998, the International Speed Post Service for both Documents and Merchandise were introduced for Belarus, Brunei Darussalam, Cuba, Fiji, Georgia, Nauru, Philippines and Taiwan.

The UPU aided International Postal Union System-96 (IPS-96) project was initiated in Delhi Circle. The system will provide track and trace facility for International Speed Post articles. The project will be extended to Mumbai, Calcutta and Chennai after the initial testing is completed.

The Export Extension Counter at Ludhiana HPO begun working w.e.f. 13.8.1998. The Export extension Counter will provide customer clearance facilities for International Outward mails and parcels. The Counter at Ludhiana is the sixth such counter to be opened after Varanasi, Kanpur, Surat, Noida and Agra.

The 28th UPU Letter-Writing Competition, commemorating the 125th Anniversary of establishment of Universal Postal Union will be held nationwide on 10th January 1999.

It is proposed to extend the Surface Air Lifted (SAL) parcel network to Austria, Morocco, Canada, Denmark, New Zealand, Sweden, Switzerland, Israel, France, Japan, Italy and Spain. The SAL Service will considerably reduce the transit time of parcels for these destination countries.

Training

Postal Staff College, India, Ghaziabad, conducted 5 induction and 9 Inservice training courses from 1.4.1998 to 31.12.1998. In all, 204 officers participated in these courses. During this period, 97 officers have been imparted training in computers also.

An International Executive Development Programme was organised from 7.12.1998 to 18.12.1998 with participation of 6 foreign officers one each from Tanzania, Nepal, Bhutan, Vietnam, Zambia and Uganda.

An Executive Development Programme exclusively for 6 officers from Bhutan would be held from 28.12.1998 to 8.1.1999, at Postal Training College, India.

In the Regional Postal Training Centres, 11,279 officials were imparted training during 1st April 1998 to 31.12.1998. Another 1967 officials were imparted training in Computers in these Regional Training Centres.

Internal work study

The work studies of PA (Admn.) of Postal Accounts Wing, Finance Advice Section and Postal Complaints Section were carried out and respective reports issued. The work-study of CPT Section has been carried out and report submitted to Finance Advice for concurrence. The work-study of PEA Section of PA Wing has also been carried out and the report is being prepared.

The study for "Evolution of norms for Group "C" staff connected with payment of pension under provisions of Coal Mines Family Pension Scheme 1971" has been completed and norms approved by S.I.U. (Staff Inspection Unit of Ministry of Finance).

Staff relations

Reverification process to recognise eligible service associations in respect of three categories of the staff viz. IPO/IRM, Assistant Accounts Officers/ Accounts Officers/Sr. Accounts Officers and PSS Group "B" Officers has been completed. The process of reverification under Central Civil Services (Recognisation of Service Association) Rules and Extra Departmental Agents (Recognisation of Association) Rules in respect of all the 9 categories of the regular employees and EDAs has been initiated.

The countrywide indefinite strike by Postal Employees held in July 1998 was effectively handled.

Staff welfare

The Postal Services Staff Welfare Board received a grant of Rs. 250.00 lakhs during 199899, out of which a sum of Rs. 55.00 lakhs has so far been released to Assam, Bihar, Uttar Pradesh and West Bengal Circles so as to provide assistance to the postal officials effected by natural calamities in these Circles.

Sports

During the period from 1st April 1998 to 31st December 1998, All India Postal Sports Board organised tournaments in Wrestling, Hockey, Football, Table Tennis, Chess, Carrom and Kabaddi. During the period 1st January 1999 to 31st March 1999, Tournaments in Cricket, Basketball, Athletics, Cycling, Volleyball, Badminton, Weightlifting, Powerlifting and Best Physique will be organised. A Cultural meet will also be organised during this period.

Recognition of higher performance

To recognise higher performance, Meghdoot Awards are given to the outstanding employees of the Department, every year. From 1998, the Department has introduced a new category to the existing 10. Categories of Meghdoot

Awards, namely Category XI - for outstanding teamwork in furtherance of a sponsored activity. The cash prize of this category is to be shared equally by the members, whereas each member will also receive a certificate. The Meghdoot Awards for 1997 and 1998 were presented in a function held on 13.10.1998. The list of the Awardees is as given below:

Awardees for the year 1997

1. Late Shri C. Veera Raju, Grade D, Kovill Patti H.O. Southern Region, Madurai, Tamil Nadu Circle
2. Late Shri B.A. Menasinakal, Postman, Laxmeshwar S.O., Gadag Division, District Dharwad, Karnataka Circle
3. Shri Mrityunjoy Shome, Sub Postmaster (HSG-II), Agartala Division, North Eastern Circle
4. Shri G.V.S.S. Sharma, Public Relations Inspector (P), Mysore, Karnataka Circle
5. Shri H. Abdul Jaleel, Sorting Assistant, APSO, Chennai, Tamil Nadu Circle
6. Shri Mohd. Walid, Sr. P.A. to Chief Postmaster General, Circle Office, Lucknow, Uttar Pradesh Circle.

Awardees for the year 1998:

1. Shri Mahabir Singh, Daftari, Regional Postal Training Centre, Saharanpur
2. Shri M.K. Khan, Senior Superintendent of Post Offices, Ludhiana City, Punjab Circle
3. Shri D.N. Sharma, Assistant Superintendent of Post Offices, Indepex '97, Delhi Circle

4.1. Shri M. Ramalingam, Assistant Director (Building), Delhi Circle

4.2 Shri S. Shanmugham, Assistant Superintendent of Post Offices, Coimbatore, Tamil Nadu Circle

4.3 Shri M Muthukrishnam, Assistant Superintendent of Post Offices, Coimbatore, Tamil Nadu Circle

4.4 Shri Ashok Kumar Sharma, Head Clerk, Delhi Foreign Post, Delhi Circle

4.5. Ms. Diana Ingty, Asstt. Manager, Speed Post Centre, Delhi Circle

The Awardees from serial nos. 4.1 to 4.5 above were awarded under category XI.

Official language

A "RAJBHASHA SAMMELAN" was organised in Bangalore (Karnataka Circle) during 1998. The Committee of Parliament on Official Language carried out inspection of Delhi GPO (Gole Dakghar), on 12.11.1998. Hindi Fortnight was organised in the Postal Directorate from 14th September 1998. Under the Rajbhasha Shield & Cash Award Scheme, 13 employees of the Directorate were awarded cash prizes for the year 1996-97, in a function held on 28.9.1998. A Hindi Workshop for Lower Division Clerks was organised in the Directorate w.e.f. 22.9.98 to 25.9.98, in which 25 LDCs took part.

12

Service Directly Under Telecom Commission

Major achievements

During the year 1997-98, a record number of 32.59 lacs new telephone connections were provided. This achievement was 22.40% more than the achievement of 25.64 lacg new connections provided during the preceding year.

Civil telephones

Telephone facilities in villages is an essential prerequisite for the development of rural sector. As against the target of 83,000 villages, 42855 villages have been covered with telephone facility during the year, bringing the total number of villages provided with telephone facilities to 310687. This represents a growth of 16 per cent over the previous year.

STD stations

The direct dialing facility is very useful for accessing distant stations instantly. The Department has, therefore, been constantly increasing the number of STD stations in the country. It was decided to increase the number of NSD/STD stations at a faster rate and, accordingly, 2799 new stations were added during 1997-98. There were 16019 NSD/STD Stations in the country as on 31.3.1998.

Accessibility

Since there is a long waiting list for telephone connections and also considering the fact that telephone facility is needed by general public who cannot afford to have a telephone of their own, it was decided that the accessibility should be improved by providing a large number of PCOs for general public. Accordingly, a total number of 210495 local PCOs, 213385 NSD/STD PCOs and 4060 High way NSD/STD PCOs have been provided up to 31.3.98.

Telephone metered call units

The number of metered call units (accounting for local and STD/ISD calls) increased to 11770.9 crores during the year compared to 9329.6 crores during 1996-97 representing an increase of 26-18%. The number of Telex metered call units declined to 9.12 crores in 1997-98 from 12.86 crores in 1996-97, representing a decrease of 29.08 %.

Rural communications

Improvement in Rural communications is evident from the following facts

Type of rural exchanges commissioned during the year 1996-97

SI. No.	Type of Equipment	No. of gross lines
1.	64 Port MILT	23494
2.	128P C-DOT RAX	113718
3.	256P C-DOT RAX	664304
4.	200L E PAM	1148
5.	512Port C-DOT SBM	121808
6.	1000L C-DOT SBM	406288
7.	1200/1400L C-DOT SBM	49396
8.	512P ILT/2048 Port ILT	38305

9.	200L E-PAM	1148
10.	Upgradation Kits (128P-256P)	81974
11.	NEAX 61/S	1524
12.	Other Exch	28822
13.	Line Module-I	101551
14.	Line Module-II,	91926
Total		1724258

Mission better communications

An intensive drive was launched under "Mission Better Communications" to enhance subscribers satisfaction by improving quality of existing services, accessibility to Telecom services in rural and urban areas, specially in hilly and backward areas through replacement of fault prone and worn-out equipments, computerisation of services, upgradation and modernisation of technology and motivational training of staff. Steps taken under "Mission Better Communications" brought fruitful results which are evident from the following:

	Target 1997-98	Achievements 1997-98
(i) Faults/100 stns/month Telephones	12.0	16.8
(ii) Trunk efficiency (%)	87.7	81.5
(iii) Call completion rate (%) (Live)		
a) Local	60.0	57.4
b) Junction	50.0	45.2
c) STD	43.0	40.5

Telecom Directorate Observation Team carried out 16 observations of telephone systems during the year. Factors which adversely affected the performance of telephone systems were analysed and brought to the notice of the concerned field units and remedial action taken. The achievements are as indicated below:

SI. No.	Activity	Achievements 1997-98	
(i)	Additions		
	Net equipped Capacity	35.19	lacs lines
	Direct Exchange Lines	32.59	lacs lines
(ii)	Accessibility		
	Total Public Telephones	427940	
(iii)	Modernisation		
	Optical Fibber Cable System commiss-	17995	RKMs
	ioned Microwave (including UHF)	23822	RKMs
	Systems commissioned		
	TAX Lines added	314.3	K
	Digital Trunk Automatic Exchanges	32	
	Digital Trunk Automatic	1251.5	K
	Exchange Lines		
(iv)	Rural CommunicationVillages provided		
	with the Telephone facility	42855	
	Small sized Electronic Exchanges	12.0 lakhs	
	Motivational Training to Staff	69084	

Financial review

Revenue expenditure and surplus

On a cash basis the revenue realisation of DOT in 97-98 (excluding Delhi and Mumbai Telephone Districts) was Rs. 14586.91 crores which includes, inter-alia Network charges from MTN Land VSNL. The net working expenses were Rs. 7554.06 crores inclusive of depreciation. The net surplus was Rs. 6746.35 crores as against Rs. 5884.95 crores in the previous year.

The status of telecommunication services as indicated by various service parameters is given below:

	Status as on	
	1.4.97	1.4.98
A) Accessibility		
—Direct Telephone Exchange Lines working (lakhs)	145.43	178.02
—Trunk Automatic Exchange	347	379
—Computerised Directory Enquiry (Station)	721	1077
—Computerised Fault Repair Service (Station)	699	1008
—Telephone facility in villages	267832	310687
—International Subscriber Trunk Dialing (ISD) facility to other countries	236	236
—Stations provided with approved NSD facility	7958	11157
—District H.Q. provided with approved STID facility	522	547
B) Quality of Service		
(a) Telephone fault rate per 100 stations per month	17.2	1.7.4
(b) Percentage delivery of telegrams within 12 day light hours	94.0	95.8
(c) Effective percentage of trunk calls	80.6	81.5

Capital investm ent

During the year the plan expenditure was Rs. 8733.57 crores and this was met from the following sources:

Internal Resources	Rs. 8733.57 crores
Market Borrowings	Nil
Budgetary Support	Nil

Out of the above plan outlay the capital investment on the fixed assets was Rs. 8646.1 0 crores. With this addition, the total investment on gross fixed assets of the Department at the end of year stood at the level of Rs. 53847.21 crores out of which dividend bearing capital is Rs. 2644.26 crores.

Tariff

— Clarification in respect of Data Circuits on Digital Transmission Media leased by DOT to Press subscribers issued vide order No.4-8/92-R&C dated 17.4.97.

— Orders for introduction of STD facility on Public Telephones provided in villages (VPTs) issued vide order No. 3-15/97-R&C dated 7.7.97

— Tariff for certain special services for Electronic Telephone Exchanges partially modified vide order No. 3-22/92-R&C dated 1.9.97.

— Clarification with regard to tariff for 64 kbps Satellite Based TDM-TDMA Network in C-Band of frequency issued vide order No. 4-10/93-R&C dated 12.11.97.

Telephone services

Access to telephone system

All the cities (300) and Towns (4689) in the country as per 1991 census have access to the telephone network through telephone exchanges.

Out of total target of 83000 villages, 42855 villages

Revenue

(Rs. in Lakhs)

	Telephone	Telex	Phone Circuit	Telegraph Circuit
(a) Total amount billed for (including MTNL) (As on 31.3.98)	1594254.00	6645.06	32723.84	3478.03
(b) Total amount collected (As on 31.3,98) Phone Telegraph Circuits Circuits	1560948.02	6855.89	30040.06	3059.51
(c) Three months old Outstanding as on 30th June, 1998	177191.78	1945.09	13440.44	3664.24
(d) Percentage of item (c) w.r.t. item (a) above (As on 31.3.98)	11.11%	29.27%	41.07%	105.35%
(e) Average Monthly Revenue during the year (including MTNL) (As on 31.3.98)	Rs. 879.36	-	-	-
(f) Percentage of excess metering complaints over the No. of bills issued during the year. (1997-98).	0.19%	-	-	-

Telex, phone circuits and telegraph circuits revenue

(Rs. in lakhs)

	Telex		Phone Circuit		Telegraph Circuits	
	1996-97	1997-98	1996-97	1997-98	1996-97	1997-98
(a) Amount billed for excluding MTNL	4942.26	6645.06	13150.02	32723.84	252.29	3478-03
(b) Amount Collected	4883.73	6855.89	12054.67	30040.06	2660.38	3059.51
(c) Three Months old outstanding as on 30th June of next financial year.	1256.30	1945.09	6946.96	13440.44	2917.73	3664.24
(d) Percentage	25.42	29.27	52.83	41.07	115.77	105.35

Telephone revenue

	Year 1996-97	Year 1997-98	%age increase
(a) Amount billed for excluding MTNL	969372.39	1170954.37	20.80
(b) Amount collected	944912.28	1147850.27	21.48

were covered with village telephone facilities during 1997-98.

1192 new telephone exchanges (net addition) were commissioned during the year raising the total number of departmental exchanges to 23392. This represents a growth of 5.36% over the previous year. The equipped capacity of telephone exchanges rose to 212.6 lakh lines with the net addition of 35.19 lakh new lines during the year representing an increase of 19.83% during the previous year.

During the year a record number of 32.59 lakh new telephone connections (Net DELs) have been added, bringing the total number of DELs to 178.00 lakhs. This represents a growth of 22.40% during the year.

Participation of private sector in basic telephone service and the licensing process

Policy provisions

In accordance with National Telecom Policy, 1994, the private operators are permitted to operate Basic Telephone Services in addition to the Department of Telecom (DOT). The monopoly position of DOT is, thus, changing to deploy where one private operator will provide Basic Telephone Services in each circle along with DOT/MTNL.

Only Indian registered companies are permitted to operate Basic Telephone Services. Foreign equity in these companies is permitted only up to 49%.

The prospective operators need to have an experience of providing 5 lakh lines of Basic Telephone Service.

The new National Telecom Policy is presently under consideration of the Government.

Achievements

Three rounds of tenders have been invited since Jan. 1995 in respect of 21 Telecom Circles in the country.

Based on these biddings 9 companies were issued Letters Of Intent (LOI) for 13 Telecom Circles. Six companies have signed the Licence and Interconnect Agreements for six circles.

Out of four companies which had filed Civil Suits in High Court of Delhi, two private companies have entered into an out of court settlement with the Government. Based on this M/s Essar Commission has already signed the Licence Agreement for Basic Telephone Service in Punjab Circle. M/s Techno Telecom, the second company, have also agreed to pay the licence fee and other required guarantees and sign the Licence Agreement.

The Court cases of two companies which were given Letters of Intent for 5 circles are still pending in the High Court of Delhi.

M/s Huges Ispat Ltd. which was issued LOIs for Maharashtra and Karnataka circles have signed the Licence for Maharashtra circle and have applied for creation of a separate legal entity for Karnataka Circle. The case is under consideration of the Government and likely to be finalised soon.

M/s Bharati Telenet Ltd., the Licensee for Basic Telephone Services in Madhya Pradesh Circle have started service in the city of Indore on 4.6.98 and in Bhopal on 9.10.98. M/s. Hughes Ispat Ltd., the Licensee for Basic Telephone Service in Maharashtra Circle has started service in Navi Mumbai on 30.10.98.

Issues raised by private operators

The Basic Service Licensees have raised various issues like deferment of IInd year Licence Fee, increasing the licence period from 15 to 25 years, relaxation of licence condition in respect of use of copper cable etc. All these issues are under consideration of a recently constituted Group on Telecommunications. These have been, resolved with the approval of the Government.

Incentives announced by the Government

Telecom Sector has been declared as "Infrastructure" with all the attendant benefits like five year Tax Holiday and after five years from the start of operations, the projects would get exemption for the balance number of years within a twelve year period. Telecom Sector would be exempt from the Minimum Alternate Tax (MAT).

The limits on External Commercial Borrowings for the Telecom projects have been made flexible, raising the ECB limits from the level of twice the equity to 50% of the Project Cost. Moreover, rupee expenditure, including the Licence Fee, has been permitted to be met from the External Commercial Borrowings.

Amortisation of Licence Fee has been permitted from the Accounting Year 1996-97. The investments made in debentures and equity shares of a public company providing telecommunication services are made eligible for tax rebate under section 88 of the Income Tax Act.

Participation of private sector in value added telecommunication services

Telecommunication has been identified the world over as a basic infrastructure essential for socioeconomic development. Modernisation and expansion of existing telecom services and introduction of new services is of utmost importance for further growth of telecommunication services in the country.

Franchise for certain value added services is being given on a nonexclusive basis. Proposals for permission/

operation of these services on a licence basis is considered by DOT for following Value Added Services:

(i) Electronic Mail Service.

(ii) Voice Mail/Audiotex Service.

(iii) Closed User Group Domestic 64 kbps Data Network Service via INSAT.

(iv) Videotex Service.

(v) Video Conferencing Service.

(vi) Credit Card Authorisation Service.

(vii) Internet.

Following services are franchised on a tender basis:

(i) Radio Paging Service.

(ii) Cellular Mobile Telephone Service.

Proposals were also invited at one time in January, 1995 for the operation of "Public Mobile Radio Trunked Service" on nonexclusive basis due to limitation in frequency spectrum in discrete service areas of 300 KMs. radius without connectivity to PSTN.

Proposals for grant of licenses for other Value-Added Services may also be considered on nonexclusive basis on submission of detailed technical and commercial proposal.

Status

(i) Electronic Mail: The licences for this service have been issued on all-India basis to 15 companies. All companies have started the operation of the service in the country.

(ii) Voice Mail/Audiotex Service:- The licence for this service is issued on a city-wise basis. Licences have been issued to 14 companies for operation of this service in 40 cities. The service has been started in 11 cities.

(iii) Closed User Group Domestic 64 kbps Data Network via INSAT The licence for the service is issued on all-India basis. 12 companies have been granted licence to operate this service. Ten companies have started operation of this service in the country.

(iv) No licence has been awarded for operation of Videotex Service, Video-conferencing and Credit Card Authorisation.

(v) Public Mobile Radio Trunked Service:- 139 License Agreements signed with 25 companies for operation of PMRTS in 54 cities are current. The service has already started in 21 cities by 17 companies.

(vi) INTERNET:- Policy for privation of INTERNET Services along with Guidelines and Terms and Conditions of the Licenses was announced in January, 1998. TRAI in its order dated 17.2.1998 has held that the INTERNET Policy formulated and announced by the Government without obtaining TRAI's recommendation regarding terms and conditions of the licenses to such service provider cannot be held valid. This has delayed the entry of private sector in the field of INTERNET Services.

(vii) Cellular Mobile Service:-The service is available in four metro cities of the country by two operators in each city. 33 Licences have been issued to 13 Indian companies for the franchise of the service in 18 Territorial Telecom Circles. The service has already started in selected cities of 17 Telecom Circles. The total number of Cellular customers in the Country are approximately 8.5 lakhs.

Telecom regulatory authority of India

The Telecom Regulatory Authority of India (TRAI) was

established through an Act of Parliament in early 1997, inter alia, to regulate the Telecom Services in the country and for matters connected therewith. As per the Act, the Authority shall consist of a Chairperson and not less than two but not exceeding six members to be appointed by the Central Government. At present, the Authority has a Chairperson and 5 members. The Head Office of the Authority is at New Delhi.

The powers and functions of the TRAI include recommending the need and timing for introduction of new service provider, the terms and conditions of licence to a service provider, ensuring technical compatibility and effective interconnection between different service providers, ensure compliance of terms and conditions of licence, and revocation of licence for noncompliance of terms and conditions of licence.

It is also required to facilitate competition and promote efficiency in the operation of telecommunications services, protect the interest of consumers of telecom services, monitoring the quality of service provided by service providers, conduct periodical survey of such services, settle disputes between service providers and ensure effective compliance of universal service obligations.

Another important function which has been entrusted to the Authority is to notify the rates at which the telecommunications services shall be provided both within and outside India.

Telephone demand

A record number of 32.59 lakhs additional new telephone connections were provided during the year 1997-98.

Quality of service

Telecom Directorate Observation Team carried out 16 observations of Telephone systems during the year.

Factors which adversely affected the performance of Telephone system were analysed and brought to the notice of the concerned field units.

Public grievances

There are several means for redressing public grievances, including Customers Service Centers, Public Grievances Cells, Telephone Adalats, Open House Sessions. During 1.4.97 to 31.3.98, 8940 complaints were received by PG Cell of Headquarters; 8518 complaints were disposed off.

Long distance services

Subscriber trunk dialing:- There has been an addition of 32 Nos. Trunk Automatic Exchanges during the year bringing the total to 379 TAXs in the country. The equipped capacity increased by 314300 lines bringing the total to 1261500 lines. The number of stations connected to the National Subscriber Dialing Network through these TAXs increased by 2799 bringing the total to 16019.

There is an increase of 26.18% in the number of telephone metered call units, the figures for the year under review being 11770.9 crores as against 9329.6 for the previous year.

Trunk services

94299 Trunk Circuits were added in the Telecom Network during the year 1997-98, bringing the total number of trunk circuits to 326851 as on 31.3.98. The percentage increase in the trunk circuits during the year was 40.54%. The number of trunk calls booked touched a total of 7.18 crores of which 5.62 crores were effective.

Computerisation of group dialing scheme

As on 31.3.97,17 ITI make SFK Digital systems (also called CTMX) were operational at various stations in the country. With further commissioning of one system each at Jodhpur, Guwahati and Agra, during the year, the figure has now gone to 20.

Implementation of group dialing scheme

As on 31.3.97, Group Dialling scheme was fully available in 1893 SDCAs in the Country. With the implementation of the scheme in another 92 SDCAs during the year, the figure has gone to 1985.

Home country direct service

In the year 1991, in association with Videsh Sanchar Nigarn Ltd. (VSNL), Home Country Direct Service was first introduced to eight countries. As on 31.3.97, this service was available for 31 countries. With the introduction of this service to Bahrain, Norway and Poland during the year, the figure has gone to 31.

"90" Service

To enable the STD barred subscribers to have an access to their District as well as Tehsil headquarters within a Long Distance Charging Area (LDCA), the Direct Dialling facility with Dynamic control and Detailed Billing using "90" as dialling code has been introduced during the year. All the Telecom Circles and Districts are making their best efforts to introduce the service in all the exchanges wherever it is technically feasible.

National sanchar doot awards

National Sanchar Doot Awards for the year 1995-96 and 1996-97 were given away to the meritorious employees of Department of Telecommunication by the Hon'ble Minister for Communication on 17.05.97, on the World Telecommunication Day. The amount of Cash Award for Sanchar Doot was also enhanced from Rs. 10,000/- to Rs. 51,000/- for each of the categories.

Transmission system

17995 RKMs of Microwave system were added with 8250 number of channels during the year. The total RKMs and total number of channels working on microwave media are 72592 RKMs and 129322 respectively at the end of the year.

23822 RKMs of optical fibre systems with 277110 channels were commissioned during the year bringing the total to 76261 RKMs and 576465 channels as on 31.3.1998.

8009 Speech channels on Open Wire Carrier Systems were commissioned during the year raising the total number of channels to 90928 as on 31.3.98.

36388 channels have been added on PCM systems raising the number of channels to 560716 as on 31.3.1998.

Wireless links

During the period 1.4.97 to 31.3.98 DOT commissioned 4 Nos. of low power point to point single channel H.F. Wireless Stations on Rent and Guarantee with a route kilometer of 506 KMs. At the end of March, 98, the total number of point to point single channel H.F. Wireless Stations were 446 with a route length of 64,000 KMs.

Telex service

Due to introduction of FAX, better STD facilities and other new technologies, telex demand is being reduced continuously. At all the stations sufficient capacities are available to meet telex on demand. The demand of telex connections is reducing day by day so much that at some places working exchanges are being closed due to withdrawal/surrendering of telex connections. In fact telex has become an obsolete technology now.

Equipped Capacity of the network has reduced from 60376 lines to 60026 lines. The number of telex working connections were 25188 as on 31st March, 1998. The number of Telex metered calls decreased to 9.12 crores during 1997-98 compared to 12.86 crores in. 1996-97 representing a decrease of 29.08%.

Public telegraph services

All the cities (300) and towns (4689) as per 1991 census and a large number of villages have access to Public Telegraph Services through Telegraph Offices.

There were 957 Departmental Telegraph Offices, 44622 Combined Offices and 981 Telecom Centres as on 31.3.1998.

Telegraph traffic

A total of 512.18 lakhs inland telegrams were booked during the year compared to 538.8 lakhs during the previous year which represents a fall of 4.94%. Of the total telegrams booked, 9.73% were on state business and 0.60% on press business.

4.09 lakhs international telegrams were booked during the period as against 5.72 lakhs in the previous year showing a decrease of 28.49% over the previous year.

Modernisation of telegraph network

— SFMS-32 lines systems was commissioned at Bhubaneswar (Orissa) on 18.5.97

— 32L SFMS at Shillong installed & kept on traffic trials.

— Five FTCS have been commissioned at Bareilly, Moradabad, Meerut, Delhi and Kanpur. Sixteen FTs in Delhi and 10 FTs in U.P.(W) have been installed.

Quality of service

95.8% of telegrams were delivered within 12 day light hours during the period 1997-98 against the yearly target of 94%.

Developmental activities

Six Telegraph Offices and seventeen Telecom Centres

were opened during the period 1997-98 and status of TOs/T.Cs. on 31.3.98 was 957/981.

Customer's facilities

Express Money Transfer Service is working well in Andhra Pradesh and Tamilnadu and now introduced in Maharashtra and Kerala circles with limited transactions within state.

Particulars of EMTs (1997-98)

i) No. of EMTs booke	
a) A. R	1,67,049
b) Tamilnadu	58,872
ii) EMT Transactions	
a) A. R	14,76,38,069
b) Tamilnadu	4,85,71,091
iii) EMT Revenue (Commission)	
a) A.R	40,14,175
b) Tamilnadu	13,96,891

Total No. of bureaufax centres on 31.12.97 was 1,283. Total no. of fax messages booked up to 31.3.98 was 32,34,466. No. of fax messages delivered (incoming fax message) up to 31.3.98 was 5,29,591. Total revenue earned from booked fax messages up to 31.3.1998 is Rs. 13,19,39,662.

Total revenue earned from incoming fax messages up to 31.3.1998 Rs. 52,35,187.

Policy matters

Decision has been taken for decentralisation of equipments used in Telegraph network and power delegated thereto.

The project for establishment of three repair centres

to maintain the SFMSS-32 lines & 64 lines (AEM make) has been approved by Telecom Commission. The Heads of circles of the concerned centres have been requested to respond to the project proposal.

The proposal of franchising of Telegraph services through franchised PCO holders stands approved by Telecom Commission in principle.

New technologies and projects of special significance

Installation of Multichannel per carrier very small aperture terminals (MCPC-VSATs). 49 number of MCPC-VSATs were made operational from 1.4.97 to 31.3.1998 at various places in country. Under this scheme, the stations which cannot be provided long distance media through terrestrial system, are provided STD facility through INSAT system. Such stations are mostly located at remote, hilly and inaccessible places including Islands having small telephone exchanges with low traffic areas.

Installation of remote area business message network (RABMN)-VSATs

Only 2 number of RABMN-VSATS were commissioned during the period 1.4.97 to 31.3.1998. These VSATs are low speed terminals and entry of private sector with High Speed Terminals have badly affected the commissioning of RABMN-VSATS. RABMN-VSATs are directly purchased by the customers from suppliers. These terminals are also able to switch on to the Telex network of the country, I-NET (i.e. terrestrial packet switched public data network) and to GPSS (i.e. Gateway Packet Switching System) for international connectivity.

Installation of high speed VSAT network (HVNET)

A satellite based network using Very Small Aperture Terminals (VSATs) to provide high speed 64 Kbps switched data service known as HVNET was made operational by 31.3.1998 along with 14 nos. of VSATs provided temporarily for Amarnath Yatra. This network also has been badly affected by the entry of private sector in this field. The network has access to DOT's Packet Switched Public Data Networks (INET/RABMN) and International data networks through the Gateway Packet Switching System of VSNL. The Network envisages voice facility amongst VSATs including connectivity to Public Switched Telephone Network (PSTN). The Hub station is co-located with satellite earth station at Mumbai.

New works

Digital satellite facility

Purchase Order was issued for supply of IDR (Intermediate Data Rate) equipment for providing digital facility at 14 stations in different parts of the country. Supply of equipment was not received during 97-98.

INSAT -Mobile Satellite Services (INSAT-MSS)

Installation of INSAT-MSS equipment had been completed at Jayanagar Earth Station (Bangalore), but service could not be commissioned due to level variation in INSAT-MSS transponder observed during Nov. 1997 which is still continuing. This system shall provide encoded voice service between land portable, maritime users & fixed users on public switched telephone network (PSTN). This shall also support data, fax, massaging & reporting services. The project is being executed by CDOT on behalf of Deptt. of Telecom. Mobile Terminals shall be purchased by the customers directly from the identified indigenous manufacturers.

Digital Circuit Multiplying Equipment (DCME)

Field trial for DCME facility to be provided at 4 stations namely Delhi, Mumbai, Calcutta and Chennai had been started at Delhi and Mumbai.

Ku-band facility

Ku-band digital facility was to be provided at 3 places namely Delhi, Bangalore and NOCC at Sikandrabad in U.P. The equipment had been procured from Ms. ISL. Antennae had been installed and alignment completed. DOT/QA testing had been completed and installation of equipments had been started at respective sites.

Data communications service

Inet Phase-II network was planned to provide data services in 89 cities, including 8 cities of Inet Phase-I. The target was extended to 102 cities. These cities have been categorised in 3 groups on the basis of business activity and demand for different types of connections and facilities. This network will have a capacity of high speed data transmission at maximum speed of up to 64 KBPs between computers as well as interactive access from public switched telephone network (PSTN).

The following were the activities for the period

(i) Type I location at Mumbai-II was commissioned.

(ii) 14 locations have been upgraded (earlier covered by ACX-40 concentrators) to type-II nodes with PSX. These are Belgaum, Chandigarh, Jabalpur, Ludhiana, Madurai, Mangalore, Mysore, Panjim, Trivandrum, Vijayawada, Bhopal, Guwahati, Patna and Vizag.

iii) Following type-III locations were commissioned:- Ahmadnagar, Ajmer, Bikaner, Durgapur, Faridabad, Gandhinagar, Gorakhpur, Haldia, Jodhpur, Kakinada, Kalyan, Karnal, Kota, Mathura, Moradabad, Muzzafarpur, Ooty, Pathankot, Quilon, Raipur, Rohtak, Rourkela, Sambalpur, Shillong, Sholapur, Siliguri, Tirupur and Trinelvelly.

Integrated Services Digital Network (ISDN)

The ISDN services have been introduced in six more cities

during this year and now the facilities are available at seventeen towns viz Hyderabad, Ranchi, Ahmedabad, Rajkot, Bangalore, Indore, Jabalpur, Pune, Nagpur, Jaipur, Tuticorin, Kanpur, Lucknow, Delhi, Mumbai, Chennai and Calcutta. The total number of ISDN subscribers at the end of March, 98 is 1211.

Introduction of Internet in Rural area - "Tele-Villages"

To commemorate the 50th Anniversary of India's Independence and to popularise and create awareness amongst the rural populace, Internet demonstration services were inaugurated in 15 rural centres, named "Tele-Villages", spread over 14 Telecom Circles on the birthday of the Father of the Nation, i.e. 2nd October, 97. These free of cost demonstrations were initially introduced for a period of three months. It was further extended by another three months. These demonstrations of Internet have been received well by the rural masses.

Major achievements in computerisation

Customer related activity

— 350 (Three Hundred Fifty) more towns have been computerised for Directory Enquiry (DO).

— 276 (Two Hundred Seventy Six) more towns have been computerised for Fault Repair Service (FRS).

— 24 (Twenty Four) more towns have been computerised for Commercial Service (CS).

Standardisation of software packages

Fault repair service (FRS) and directory enquiry (DO):- COMMANDIR Package for Fault Repair Service (FRS) & Directory Enquiry Services (DQ), standardised by *DOT,* has been implemented in 222 SSAs for Directory Enquiry and in 219 SSAs for Fault Repair Service. The COMMANDIR Package for DQ services has been tested for ten lacs lines with 150 operators under simulation conditions. The Package has also been modified and its upgraded version 1.3.1 has been released by TEC, which contains number of new features like import of data from Commercial Service etc.

Nation wide directory enquiry services (NDQ):- As decided in 1995 to implement ONLINE Nation Wide Directory Enquiry Service using X-25 and X-28 INET connections. 127 SSAs have been provided Host connectivity with data of whole SSAs.

Computerised commercial service system (CSS):- Commercial Service System (CSS) Package developed at Chandigarh by M/s dde-ORG have been modified to incorporate additional features and ver. 1.2 has been validated.

The Package has been made over to C-DOT for maintenance, upgradation, integration with other Packages and for distribution to field units.

The instruction Manual for installation & operation of CSS Package was prepared and circulated to the field units. The guidelines for Acceptance Testing (A/T) of the CSS package by T&D circle were prepared & circulated to the field units.

Regular Training is being imparted in this package. During this period, six training courses have been organised at BRBRAITT Jabalpur. Training in SCO UNIX and ORACLE is also being imparted.

Computerisation of TR builling and accounting (TRBA):- Trichur package for TR Billing and Accounting (Trichur), Standardised in DOT, has been made over to C-DOT along with source code and documentation for further maintenance, development and integration of this package with other customer related packages.

Inventory management:- Inventory Management

Package for use in CTS and CSD has been tested and Version 1.1 has been standardised for implementation in CTSs/CSD. A Steering Committee constituted under the Chairmanship of Advisor (production), Telecom Commission completed its work and submitted its report. The package (IMTC) has already been implemented in 7 CTSs/CSDs and it is under implementation at other places. The Draft specifications for procurement module for CGM TS, Calcutta and MM Cell of DOT has been finalised for making over to C-DOT for the development of software package.

Software for project management:- MS Software package for Project Management has been standardised for use in DOT 40 copies of the software have been purchased and distributed one copy each to all field units. Training to field staff has been imparted for its use.

Computerised Facilitation Counters:- As a measure of responsive and effective administration, it has been decided by the Cabinet Secretary to set up Computerised Facilitation Counters (CFC) at the Reception of all the Ministries/Departments of the Government of India for disseminating information to the citizen/user regarding schemes/procedures of the organisation, forms and applications, and about individual applications.

CFC at the Reception of Sanchar Bhawan has been made operational. All the Telecom Circles and PSUs of DOT have been asked to setup similar CFC at their Headquarters, in response of which CFC has already been made operational at the HQ of Maharashtra Telecom Circle and Kerala Telecom Circle and at other places action is being taken to set up such Facilitation Counters.

Interactive voice response system (IVRS).- Rajasthan Telecom Circle, who had been nominated for the development of Software for Integrated Interactive Voice Response System (IVRS), has awarded the tender for development & implementation of Software at Alwar, as a pilot project. The Company has developed the software and TEC/C-DOT has been asked to validate the software. The software is expected to be available for distribution to the field units during the first quarter of 1998-99.

Integrated Customer Management Software Package:- TEC/C-DOT has recently tested an Integrated Software Package "AP-SOFT" for DQ, TRB&A and Commercial Service System. This package is being developed indigenously by AP Telecom Circle.

Zonal meeting in computerisation:- Four Zonal Meetings were organised under the Chairmanship of Adv(T) in New Delhi, Mumbai, Chennai and Calcutta during the year, in which all the field units participated, for reviewing the progress in computerisation and to discuss various problems being faced both in the computer Hardware and software front.

Workshop in Computerisation:- Two workshops were organised during the year by Information Technology Cell, one for TRA Billing at C-DOT Bangalore and another on Computerisation at ALTTC, Ghaziabad to discuss computerisation in DOT.

Activities in Sanchar Bhavan

(i) LAN Server working in Sanchar Bhawan and Dak Bhawan have been upgraded to Pentium Pro. Connectivity between Sanchar Bhavan and Dak Bhavan Server has been established.

(ii) During the period 39 more Pentium PCs, printers & 5 servers have been added and another 53 Pentium PCs with latest MS Office '97 software is being procured.

(iii) Computerisation Gate Pass has been introduced at the Reception of Sanchar Bhawan to issue gate pass to visitors since Dec. 97.

(iv) DOT-MAIL facility has been made operational in the Sanchar Bhawan through which data and file can be transferred. E-mail facility is also available through Internet on DOT-MAIL.

(v)Admn. IV section has been selected as one of the sections in TCHQ for full computerisation working. For this a private vendor "Prodata" has completed the system study, the report of which is under approval.

(vi) Microsoft Corporation of India Ltd. has been associated for system study of TCHQ working with an objective of bringing Office Automation and modernising the way of working in Telecom Directorate.

(vii) A Quarterly News Letter on Information Technology has been started from the IT Cell to disseminate the information on Information Technology. First issue of this News Letter has been published and distributed in Feb., 98.

(viii) Additional Books on computer and IT has been added in the computer library for use of the Officers of DOT A list of computer books available in the Computer Library is made available on LAN for accessing by the users.

(ix) The report of the Committee set up for scrapping, the old version computers of the type PC XT286/ PCAT-286 working in Telecom Directorate has been finalised. Case is being processed to replace the old Computers of configuration - PC AT/286 and its earlier versions.

(x) Internet Connections are being provided to all senior officers, of the level of IDDG & above of Telecom Directorate.

(xi) LAP-TOP Computers are being procured for providing to Senior officers of Telecom Commission.

Future plan

(i) Standardisation of Integrated Package for Customer related service like Commercial Service, TRBA, DO, FRS etc.

(ii) Establishment of Call Center.

(iii) Upgradation of LAN at TCHQ, New Delhi.

(iv) Creation of DOT web site and Wide Area Network.

(v) Creation of Multimedia Center.

(vi) Computerisation of Material Management System of DOT by development of a Software package for Procurement Module of Accounting modules of M. M. System.

(vii) Replacement of old Computers and Printer Working in Telecom Directorate and providing state of art Pentium Computers, Printer, UPS and latest Software for office working.

C-DOT

Projects in the field

MAX-XL:- The infrastructure assessment for M/s ITI was completed by QA and the type approval was given to Mis. ITI. After commissioning of Indira Nagar exchange, the MAX-XL switches are now being installed at more sites namely, Bihar (Madhubani), Karnataka (Chikmaglur, Yelahanka, Gadag, Mandya)), Tamil Nadu (Dindigal, Namakkal, Kumbakonam, Nagercoil), Kerala (Affingal), Punjab (Abhor). TOT training program was completed for nine more manufacturers namely, BEL, BHEL Crompton Greaves, Keltron, IL-Kota, Hindustan Teleprinters, Punjab Communication, United Telecom and ECIL. Order for two lakh lines of MAX-XL exchanges (including 40K lines for Jayanagar, field trial site with ISDN and 800 K BHCA capability) was placed with the M/s Indian Telephone Industries (ITI). So far, 10 exchanges (One lakh lines) were commissioned in the field.

Technology for C-DOT SBM-RAX based on "XL" hardware and MAX-XL has also been offered to the C-DOT switching products manufacturers.

ISDN CPEs:- Functional evaluation of ISDN customer premises equipment, namely, Network Termination (NT310) and Terminal Adapter (TA210) by TEC was completed successfully and TEC approval has been accorded. The interworking of these equipment with all the new technology exchanges has been satisfactorily proven Technology transfer for NT310 and TA210 to M/s ITI model plant was completed.

TAX-XL:- The TAX-XL at Ratfam was commissioned with CCS #7 signalling towards OCB TAX at Bhopal and Siemens EWSD TAX at Indore. Bhopal TAX was synchronized with national clock and the field trial was completed successfully.

CCS #7 SIGNALLING SYSTEM:- CCS #7 (SS7) field trial for MAX-L was completed at Kharagpur. Environmental tests of Signalling Unit Module (SUM) were also carried out at Bangalore C-DOT SBM RAX MAX-L and MAX-XL exchanges have become capable of supporting IN and ISDN services.

Non A/C RSU:- The development of non-A/C RSU (Remote Switching Unit) capable for QM333 category B operation was completed. After the successful field trials at Ratnagiri (Maharashtra and Vapi (Gujarat), TEC clearance was obtained.

Detailed billing and bulk billing:- The detailed billing and bulk billing facilities on junctions for C-DOT exchanges were tested satisfactorily. The bill monitoring software package was developed, tested and TEC clearance was obtained after successful field trials.

Network Synchronization Equipment (NSE):- The Network Synchronization Equipment (NSE) developed for level 2 operation in the synchronization network was successfully tested for clock stability and jetters transfer function by TEC. This equipment fully satisfies ITU-T standards and can be used for network synchronization of E-10B and C-DOT SBM RAX, as well as MAX-L exchanges. The equipment was offered to TEC and after field trial with E-10B exchanges clearance for production has been obtained Transfer of Technology is in progress to M/s ITI, Mankapur.

Regional access barring ('90') facility:- Testing of regional access barring '90' facility in C-DOT exchanges (256P RAX/SBM/RAX/MAX-L/MAX-XL) was completed by TEC. C-DOT organized 30 workshops in different telecom circles and about 900 DOT officials were trained on retrofitting the facility The new versions of the software are being ported on all the existing exchanges in the field.

SBM RAX:- With the commissioning of 317 exchanges (4.68 lakh lines) during the year, the total number of the same commissioned in the field so far has gone up to 2300 exchanges (21.64 lakh lines).

MAX-L:- With the commissioning of 47 exchanges (2.97 lakh lines) during the year, the total number of the same commissioned in the field so far has gone up to 310 exchanges (12.53 lakh lines).

256P RAX

— Country adaptations for Ethiopia, Colombia, Gambia,

Bangladesh were completed. RAX software version (DOT version) 2-1 -1 was released with following enhancements

— Dynamic O/G restriction matrix.

— Regional STD (90) facility

— STD/ISD restrictions on CCB subscribers.

— Total number of RAXs (256P & 128P RAX) operational in the network is 19,000.

TDMA PMP:- The validation of the equipment including environmental testing was completed by TEC. The field trial of the equipment was successfully completed with Mysore as a base station and remotes; at Harohalli, Doora and Varuna. After the formal technology approval the equipment would be ready for bulk production.

MCPC VSAT:- The MCPC VSAT equipment in C-Band was evaluated by TEC. The equipment was installed for a field trial with hub at Jaynagar and remote at Maralwadi (Bangalore).

INSAT mobile satellite system (INSAT MSS):- This project was undertaken for providing mobile satellite services through indigenous satellite INSAT-2C. Hub equipment, portable and maritime terminals were developed jointly to meet these requirements by C-DOT and COMSAT laboratories of USA. The installation and testing of the system was completed at Jayanagar, Bangalore with satellite simulator and INSAT 2C satellite during its availability. The system supports voice, data and fax communication between the mobile terminals and also between mobile and PSTN subscribers with hub as gateway. The transfer of technology (TOT) process for these terminals to the indigenous manufacturers is proposed after commissioning.

Progress in the development of key projects

Integrated services digital network (ISDN):- C-DOT has developed Integrated Services Digital Network (ISDN) capability for its exchanges. The ISDN interfaces, bearer services and supplementary services have been developed according to ITU-T and national standards. The basic functions of ISDN interfaces, supplementary services, fax, and video calls were demonstrated to the Telecom Commission during August, 1997. The ISDN capability can be retrofitted on existing exchanges by deploying the ISDN Terminal Unit (ISTU) in addition to SS7 Signalling Unit Module (SUM).

Intelligent Network (IN) Services

Service logic was develop for Service Control Point (SCP) for creation of a number of services using SSP on C-DOT switches. IN services hold immense value-addition and revenue earning potential for the service providers. Besides, the subscribers would be able to get improved service flexibly and economically.

The trial for SSP (SSP functionality implemented in C-DOT SBM Exchange) with Toll - Free Phone Service was launched in MTNL (Delhi) network at Karol Bagh on the occasion of the 50th Anniversary of India's Independence and subsequently in Calcutta Network. The toll-free phone service aims at providing the subscribers charge-free access to MTNL officers. IN services based on C-DOT technology are now proposed to be provided at Ahmedabad, Chennai, Bangalore, Hyderabad, Jaipur, Lucknow, Patna and Pune.

V 5.1/5.2 interface for C-DOT Switches:- C-DOT worked on V5.2 interface which is an emerging concept for connecting Access Network Product (ANP) to the main exchange. This interface can serve different type of interfaces including radio system of the "Wireless In Local Loop (WILL)".

C-DOT is implementing the standardized protocols related to V 5. 1 /V 5.2 to interface access network with C-DOT switches. This will help in interconnecting various access technologies to C-DOT exchanges. Currently, the product is under system validation and its interface with C-DOTs composite MUX to provide remoting features for POTs and ISDN (basic rate) subscribers has been established in the lab.

Composite MUX (remote line concentrator):- A 120 line unit is under development which will serve both analog and ISDN subscribers. This remote line concentrator has connection to the C-DOT main exchange or remote BM (Base Module) using V 5.2 interface. Another version of the unit with V 5.1 interface can function as a multiplexer. The equipment will be available in two versions- Wall mounted and Desktop.

Asynchronous transfer mode (ATM) system:- The Asynchronous Transfer Mode (ATM) is an emerging technology for meeting broadband transmission and switching requirements. The first prototype ATM cross-connect switch has been designed.

Fibre access system (FAS):- Lab realization work progressed further. The equipment would provide Fibre To The Curb (FTTC) and Fibre To The Home (FTTH) solutions in the access part of the telecom network. Some hardware sub modules were tested and other modules are in various stages of design. Software subsystems are under development.

Synchronous digital hierarchy (SDH) system:- These projects constitute a series of products namely, STM-1, STM-4, Digital Access Cross-connect (DACCS) and Network Management System. The development of these products are in different stages of product cycle. While, the STM is in the internal validation stage, the STM-4 and DACCS are in the lab realization stage.

Digital Enhanced Cordless Technology (DECT) System:- This system provides Wireless In the Local Loop (WILL) solutions both in the urban and in the rural scenarios. While on solution uses Base Station Controller (BSC), Base Station Units (BSU) and remote radio units, the other uses an interface card in the remote line of the TDMA system the later can serve wireless subscribers instead or wired subscribers usually supported by TDMA. Both the systems are in the final stages of lab integration.

Field & manufacturing support

To reassure its manufacturers on C-DOT support, many workshops and discussions were held with the manufacturers. C-DOT continued to provide product support to 21,000 switches with 5.8 million lines of C-DOT technology in the network in terms of upgradation, retrofitting and training to field staff. C-DOT continued its interaction with the manufacturers and field installations for providing all types of maintenance support.

TEC clearance received

Bulk production clearance was received for ASIC Based Signal Processing (ISP - Integrated Signal Processing) card after field trial at Ambala and other sites in Haryana. This card will replace the existing Signalling Processor Card (SPC) being used in 256P RAX, SBM RRAX, MAX-L and MAX-XL.

Bulk production clearance was received for high performance version of existing IOP (after field trials at Haldwani MAX-L) used with SBM RAX, MAX-L and MAX-XL exchanges (IOP-VII) developed with the entire control circuitry implemented on a single PCB and more powerful CPU. This will make the equipment more reliable and easy to maintain.

Clearance for the S/W link 1-4-5.43-3 was received after successful field trials at Hoshiarpur (MAXL) Dasua

(MAX-M) and Indira Nagar (MAX-XL). Some of the features supported in the link are:

— Regional ('90' level) barring.

— 16 PCM connectivity between RSU and the main exchange.

— IOP booting from the unix cartridge.

Clearance for the S/W link 1-4-2.25-4 was received after successful field trials at Sonepat (Haryana). Some of the features supported in the link are :

— Metering and detailed billing on junctions.

— Call saving on bus failure.

— Calling line identification.

— Centralised Automated Message Accounting (CAMA).

Clearance for the S/W link 1-4-8.1-3 was received after successful field trials at Ratlam (M.P.) and Kharagpur (West Bengal). The release supports

— SS7 and Network Synchronisation

— Clearance was received for SBM RAX based on "XL" hardware.

— Non-A/C RSU was accorded clearance after successful field trial.

— Technology approval was accorded for C-DOT NSE (Network Synchronisation Equipment) after successful field trial for use as standalone equipment in E-10B exchanges.

— Technology approval was accorded for C-DOT NSC (Network Synchronisation Controller) after, successful field trial for integration and use in C-DOT MAX-XL and TAX-XL exchange configurations.

— Clearance for the SM link 2-1 -1 was received for 256P RAX.

— ESL card supporting 16 PCM connectivity between the main exchange and the RSU (MAX-L) was given clearance.

— Functional clearance was received for Enhanced Subscriber Unit (ESU), used as Calling Line Identification (CLI) unit with PC interface.

— Clearance was received for ISDN CPEs (Customer Premises Equipment) namely, NT310 (Network Termination) and TA210 (Terminal Adapter).

— Clearance was obtained for propagating COMAC (Centralise Operation and Maintenance Centre) software package for 256PRAX in field.

— Clearance was obtained for propagating BMON (Bill Monitoring) software package for bill monitoring function for MAX.

Standards and specifications

GRs finalised:- PTC Thermistor for use on MDF; Digital Loop Carrier System (DLC) on SDH; Bill Processing system for INET Phase II; Frame Relay switch; Router; Internet Service Provider; Frame Relay Access Device; Smart Card Payphones; Smart Card Pay Phone Control Unit; Smart Card Pay Phone Management System; Boss-Secretary Telephone System; Pocket sized Card Reader for Smart card Payphone systems; Key Telephone System; Intelligent Network Application Part-National standard; NT1 for interface approval; C-DOT Trunk Automatic Exchange-XL; Noise Figure Meter; Digital Radio Measurement System; Stand Alone Synchronisation Equipment; Electromagnetic Compatibility Standard; Multi Protocol Frame Relay Concentrator; Managed Leased Line Network; 2048 KBPS Line Driver;

ATM/Frame Relay Protocol Analyser; Aerial Optical Fibre; National Internet Backbone; Store and Forward Fax Service; Line Jack Unit; Indian Script Code for Language Paging; Indian Script Code for Language Paging Devanagri/Marathi; Indian Script Code for Language Paging Gujarati; Subscriber Service Unit for calling Line Identification Purpose.

GRs revised/amended/Errata:- Saddles for fitting Cl brackets and struts of tublars poles; Angle Iron Ties; Caps for tublar poles; Mole Skin; Iron line stores; Bracket and Plastic insulated telephone stalk; HDPE pipes; Brace Angle Iron; Saddle for fitting Angle Iron Guard Bracket on Hamilton Tubes A & B; Coupling of different types of Clamp for couplings; 10/20 pair DP with 10 pair Quick connection (IDC) Drop wire module and casing; GD Tubes for Internal/External use; FRP Moulded DP Box 10 & 20 pairs with moulded tag block; Discrete Connectors, Intelligent Network Services; TR Billing Hardware; VSAT based distance Education system; V.32 bis modem card; Voice band data modem (V.29); ISP equipment dimensioning/configuration; Amendment No.1 to Single pair/10 pair Screened PCM Cable for Inter bay digital equipment wiring; Additional climatic and environmental tests for Electronic Push Button Telephone for 98-99 procurement; ISDN Customer Premises Equipment; Large size local cum Tandem Digital Switching system; National routing, switching and numbering plan; Wireless local loop System; PCM MUX equipment; 2/ 8 Mb/s Direct Digital MUX; Third Order Digital MUX. equipment; Fourth Order Digital MUX. equipment: 2/34 Mb/s Direct Digital MUX; MDF for 512 lines and above; Commercial System; TR Billing and Accounting System.

GRs withdrawn:- Cable paper core unit twin lead sheathed armoured; Cable paper core star quad trunk armoured; Cable paper core star quad local armoured;

Cable paper insulated PE sheathed Al moisture barrier with steel tape armouring and PE jacket; Cable lead sheathed PCUT PE protected un-armoured; Copper wire for UG cable 1955 spec.; Insulating or wrapping paper used in telephone cables; Lead sheath for UG telephone cables; Steel tapes used in UG telephone cables; Jute (hessian cloth) used in dry Core telephone cables; Bitumen base filling compound; Copper strips for wires, copper and copper weld; House Bracket; Compression sleeve for making crimped joint for 2.12 mm GI wire and drop wire; RCC sockets forming the bottom sockets - section of hamilton poles; CT Box Intl 6 pairs; Cable Terminal Box 20 pairs External; Asbestos cement ducts; Self supporting PVC Drop Wire with integral barrier; PE insulated and sheath with GI wire as integral barrier; Voice band data modem (V.29); 2400/1200/300 bps voice band data modem cards with addendum; Videotex terminal; Add-on unit to Coin box Telephone (CBT-80); Single Channel VHF system; 2/15 Shared Radio System (Issue-02); 2/15 Shared Radio System (Issue-04); 4/36 Analogue MARR; Development spec. for PCM cable for 2 Mb/s digital line; Development spec. for PCM cable for 2 MB/s digital system; Programming Loading Coil; General specification for all testing instruments; Digital Multimeter; Base Band Data Modem; STD Coin Collection Box; Line Jack Unit for Termination Telephone Line amendment; Quarter Modular Line Cord; Electronic Telephone Instrument; Add on Unit to Coin Box Telephone; Card Vending Machine; Disposable Smart Card; Monitoring and Control System for Direct Exchange Line.

Engineering guidelines issued for:- Frame Relay Service through Inet Phase II; Integration of INET Phase-I equipment into INET Phase II network; For X.75 gateway for connecting other Data networks to Inot: PSTN Access Procedure in Inet Phase 11; Digital Satellite Phone

Terminal (DSPT); CCS-7 implementation; Internet connectivity for DOT, Space/power requirements for ATM equipment; 18 GHz Digital M/W system; "90" dialling scheme within LDCA; INMARSAT-VPT numbering, routing plan; Switching and Routing Plan for Cellular Mobile Telephone Services.

Test schedule prepared for:- SDH Analyser 1/4/16; NT interface approval; SSU (Subscriber Service Unit); CLIP (Calling Line Identification Presentation); ISDN Customer Premises Equipment; PTC Thermistor; FRP DP Box 10/20 pairs with moulded tag block; ISDN Protocol tester; 16 KHz Metering PUIse Analyser; Key Telephone System; CMTS Monitoring for circles; Point of interconnection test; Public Mobile Radio Trunking Service; Cellular Mobile Telephone Services; Network Termination Equipment; Installation of Accessory and Fixure for installation of self Supporting Metal Free Aerial Optical Fibre Cable; Terminal Adapter; Multipath Fade Simulator; IR between PSTN and Network of licensed service providers interface at 2048 kbps.

Testing, field trial and validation of new technology system and products

Barring and detailed billing for 90/98 level in C-DOT SBM, RAX and MAX-L exchange and for level 90 in new technology exchanges; Software link 1-4-5, 43-3 supporting dynamic barring and detailed billing over level 90 for C-DOT, SBM, MAX-L, MAX-XL exchange; C-DOT MAX-XL software with link 1-4-8.1-3 with dynamic barring and detailed billing for level 90; C-DOT ISP and IOP card; Synchronisation of C-DOT MAX-XL exch. to increase the modem Data rate of Subs; C-DOT exch. for bill monitoring functionality (BMON), C-DOT NSE 2.0 (Network Synchronisation Equipment); Non-A/C RSU of CDOT, CLI P facility in C-DOT MAX-L at Sonepat with software Link 1-4-2.25-4; 16 PCM RSU connectivity for

C-DOT MAX-L; Environmental testing of C-DOT Network Synchronisation Equipment (NSE); Environmental testing on CCS-7 unit of C-DOT, Technology approval for C-DOT-NSC (Networking Synchronisation Controller) in MAX-XL exchanges; 10 digit CLI in FETEX 100L switching system; Software patch for 1/3 tariff for FETEX 150; Pending points of validation in 5ESS Exchange; Tandem working for 5ESS system; PRI interface in 5ESS; Software patch in EWSD switching systems; Software version 9 in EWSD local exchange; ISDN PC card of M/s CMC; Line parameter measurements on ISDN lines; CCS7 and ISDN interworking of NEAX-61 E; International ISDN; national and International roaming for Mobile Services; IIT developed WLL system based on DECT Technology; Field trial of DECTWLL system of M/s Ericsson at New Delhi; VSAT services; Ku band Hub Station Equipment except HPA in association with QA at ISL, Bangalore tested; STM-4 in ring Configuration and Point to Point of M/sAlcatel at Hyderabad; ADM-1 of M/s Fibcom. completed; ADM-4 of M/s Fibcom. Gurgaon; Field trial of STM-16 of M/s Fibcom at Bombay; Optical fibre Splicing machine of M/s Seven Hills Optic Communication, Calcutta; Pending points of CDTMX at Chennai; New features of CTMX system of ITI; Testing of AMS (Alarm Management System), DEL (Digital Error Logger) and DPM (Digital Performance Monitoring) in the Telestra NMS system at Chennai; Voice Mail/Audiotex services of M/s Sawarkar Telecom Pvt. Ltd.; Video conferencing over ISDN at 128 Kbps between TEC, N.D. and BRBBRAITT, Jabalpur; Video Conferencing at 364 Kbps; CSMS (Customer Services Management System) offered by MTNL at Bhikaji Cama Place for commercial and billing modules; Credit Card Authorisation service; 20 GHz Signal Generator and VSWR test set of M/s Meera Agencies; Frame Relay Access Device (FRAD) of M/s PCL, New Delhi; 2.7 GHz synthesized Signal Generator of M/s HP India; ISDN feature Phone in OCB-283 and F-150 exchanges; New features for EWSD technology against 1.3 m tender; Validation of NEAX-61 E exchange at Modinagar; Validation of FETEX-1 50 exchange Version 4.0 for CCS7, Supplementary Services, Charge Band and ILT features; STM-1 6 of M/s Fibcom; Chandigarh Commercial System; Commercial modules and TRA modules of APSOFT of A.P Telecom Circle at Hyderabad; Digital Line Concentrator of M/s MIC; C-DOT SBM RAX based on XL hardware with software 1-4-5.43-3 with IOP-VH; Validation software developed by Indore Telecom District for recording of traffic measurements in EWSD TAX on hourly basis for CCR study; DCME equipment installed between Delhi and Mumbai; C-DOT, TDMA-PMP system; WLL, CDMA technology field trial; Validation of 11 GHz, 140 Mbps Microwave equipment of M/s NATELCO Nasik.

Network planning/engineering

Planning of PON network based on optical fibre technology in rural communication; Proposal identified to provide reliable Telecom Services to the rural sector with high demand and potential growth at Ludhiana Telecom Distt.; Memorandum to Telecom Commission in respect of pilot project on "Distance Learning and Remote Library access" as Asia Pacific Telecommunity Bangkok Project prepared; Engineering guidelines for x TDMA PMP System; Data Analysis for the Propagation Measurement at Mumbai; New Humidity and Temp. Sensor procured from USA tested at Chingelputte; Data Analysis for the Propagation Measurement at Mumbai.

Field support

Distributed COMMANDIR package to various places and provided support for installation; Enquiry Module of Commandir (2 Exch. Ver.) modified as per the requirements given by Bhavnagar Telecom Distt.;

Synchronisation of OCB Jullandhar with OCB TAX Karolbagh, N.Delhi; Synchronisation of Bhopal OCBTAX with Bombay EWSDTAX and OCI3 TAX Karolbagh, N.Delhi; Supplied IMA Ves. MS software of El OB exchange to different places; Distributed E-1 OB maintenance Advisor package to various field units; Developed and tested and provided assistances for implementing E-10B software for 8 digit depth analysis; Provided technical support in E-10B upgradation of 2L version software; Supplied Exec., Real data and SDF tapes to Chirala, Okhla and Pathankot El OB exchanges; Provided technical assistance in upgration of local EWSD exch. at CUFF Prade to patch status 17V; Implemented upgraded software in EWSDTAX at Raipur and Ahemdabad; Modified FOCIN command for Network Management System implemented at Delhi Gate exch. for field trial; CCS7 introduced between Ratlam, Bhopal and More; Instructions on ISDN testing; CLIP software supplied to Calcutta Telephones; BNRC (Back up National Reference Clock Centre) at Karol Bagh, handed over to MTNL, New Delhi; Issued Implementation procedure of CLI in E10B exchange; Status of CCS7 links in New Technology exchange consolidated addressed.

Field problem solved

International ISDN access from Kanpur; Call failure on C7-R2 interworking at Bhopal OCB-283 DTAX; Analysis of nature of Address indicator in OCB Tandem Exchange-, CCS7 interworking between EWSD MSG and OCIB -Tandern; Creating CCS-7 signalling link over satellite media in OCB TAX Calcutta; CCS7 interworking between C-DOT, SEIM and OCB 283 exchanges at Shimla; Signalling Transfer Point (STP) function introduced in MTNL Delhi Network for CCs-7 working in AXE-10 exch. at Nehru Place; in EWSD TAX at Ahemdabad; Disconnection of Dial tone at Delhi Gate E1013 exch.; False alarm from BT rack at Nehru Place El

08 exch.; Non-functioning of status for dynamic STID at Jammu E10B exch.; For OCHALA printout at E-10B exchange Bhatinda; Creation of new file by data correction in MTR file at E-1 08 Guwahati exchange; Corruption in ADB in E-10B exchange Dehradun by data correction in TR files; Restored DI Nehru Place exchange OMC by using OMC backup; File creation at Dilshad Garden E-10B exchange Delhi by data correction in catalogue file; Prepared Exec. tape for Hoshiarpur E-1 OB exchange; Unstable link between E-10B exchange and OMC at Gorakhpur; Non-supression of Directory nos. and wrong announcement on incoming calls at Karolbagh E-10B exch.; Initialisation of TR due to corruption in Catalogue file solved by disk data correction in E-10B Kanpur; Creation of SR5 subscriber due to corruption in TMNE file solved by OMC data modification in E-10B Kotakapura.

Tender evaluation

Procurement of solid state disk drive/Winchester drive for the replacement of UD50 disk drive at E-10B software centre; Procurement of PCM analyser; Procurement of software for TEC LAN; Assisted Telecom Commission in evaluation of the tender 6 GHz and 11 GHz SDH Microwave equipment; ADB tender for Rural communication for Eastern U.P; For procurement of Line Drivers and stand alone enclosure; Procurement of UPS system and laser printer; Assisted MTNL Delhi in evaluation of the tender for Managed Leased Data Network (MLDN); Router; 1.69 million line tender for local exchange.

Other activities

13 GHz 34 Mbps digital radio system installed at MTNL Mumbai; Impact of Y2 K problem in DOT reviewed; Technical paper prepared on "Spectrum issues for Radio based PCS"; Test report for Roaming in CMTS using STP

sent to VAS cell; Seminar on ISDN, OCB 283, ATM, INET and SDH Network on Video Conferencing between BRBRAITT Jabalpur and New Delhi as part of distance learning; List of specifications and equipments finalised for Multimedia Project; Multimedia Kit installation completed; Presentation on TEC LAN on UTP demonstrating access to TEC Web pages on Intranetware, Unix Server and Internet was given at TEC computer Lab. to ADET Trainees of ALTTC Ghaziabad; Multiparity Video Conferencing demonstration among TEC Delhi, MTNL Bombay, TTC Jabalpur and Bangalore Telephone District; Updated the Internet TEC Web Pages; Analysis of Ku band propagation data for calculation of Annual exceedance and worst month statistics completed; Seminar on ATM was organised at Bombay, in coordination with MTNL, Bombay; Specifications for Pentium PCs, Laserjet, Printers, Modems and UPS System; The PSX loaded with new software release supporting Frame Relay and their configuration updated at ALTTC; Modified guidelines for Inet Ph I and Ph II connectivity and sent for field trial.

Comments provided on

National Preparatory Committee (NPC) to the World Radio Communication Conference; Final report of the working group on fixed services for allocation of exclusive bandwidth for higher density fixed services in 40 GHz and 50 GHz band.

Type approval issued

Type Approvals	646
Interface Approvals	318
Source/Compatibility Approval	23
Service Test Certificates	268

Telecom factories

The Telecom factories previously known as P&T

Workshops are as old as Indian Telegraph itself. The oldest workshop was set up at Alipore, Calcutta as a repair workshop in 1855. It gradually started production of Telegraph and Telecom equipments required by the Department. At present there are seven Telecom Factories located at Mumbai, Calcutta (Alipore & Gopalpur), Jabalpur (Wright Town & Richhai), Bhilai and Kharagpur. The factories are Central Government units like Ordnance factories and Railway workshops.

Production

The main products of the factories are as under

(a) Telecom factory, Mumbai

(i) C.D. Cabinets

(ii) C.T Box

(iii) Support Bracket

(iv) Private Wire Relay Set

(v) D.P. Box

(vi) MDFs

(vii) Line Jack Units

(viii) Modems

(ix) Electronic Relay Plates

(x) Pay Phones

(b) Telecom factory, Culcutta (Alipore)

(i) Bracket Channel Iron

(ii) Buttenski Telephone

(iii) C.D. Cabinets

(iv) C.TBox

(v) D.P.Box

(vi) Line Jack Units

(vii) MDFs

(viii) Microwave Towers/TTH Tower

(ix) Mast 40/15 Meter

(x) Personal Computer (Supply and Maintenance)

(xi) Repair of E-1 OB/C-DoT Cards

(xii) Repair of Telephone Instruments

(xiii) Stalks

(xiv) Support Bracket

(xv) U-Back

(c) Telecom factory, Calcutta (Gopalpur)

(i) Galvanising Operation

(ii) Microwave Towers

(iii) Masts

(d) Telecom factory, Kharagpur

(i) Sockets.

(ii) Sole Plates

(iii) Saddles.

(iv) Special Alloy Castings for Exports

(e) Telecom factory, Jabalpur (wright town)

(i) Tubes (Riveted).

(ii) Bracket Channel Iron.

(iii) Stalks.

(iv) C.D.Cabinets.

(v) Line Jack Units.

(vi) Microwave Towers/TTH Towers

(vii) Repair of C-DOT Cards

(viii) Masts 40/15 Meter

(ix) Repair of Telephone Instruments

(x) Support Bracket

(xi) U-Back

(f) Telecom factory, Jabalpur (Richhai)

(i) Tubes (Welded)

(ii) Galvanising Operation

(g) Telecom factory, Bhilai

(i) Microwave Towers/TTH Towers

(ii) Mast 15 Meter

Telecom factories are under the charge of Chief General Managers in Senior Administrative Grade. CGM, Telecom factory, Mumbai is incharge of Mumbai factory. CGM, Telecom factory, Jabalpur is incharge of Wright Town (Jabalpur) and Bhilai Units. CGM, Telecom factory, Calcutta is incharge of Alipore, Gopalpur & Kharagpur Units. CGM, Telecom factory, Richhai is incharge of Richhai (Jabalpur) unit.

Staff strength

The staff strength of the factories as on 31-3-98 is as the next page:-

Unit (TF)	Gr'A'	G r'B'	Gr'C'	G r'D'	Sub-Total	Indus-trial	Total
Mumbai	17	2B	287	117	449	1096	1545
Alipore	13	26	267	134	440	1106	1546
Gopalpur	2	4	12	1	19	96	115
Kharagpur	6	10	31	23	70	261	331
Wright Town	16	22	197	132	367	994	1361
Richhai	11	11	67	58	147	478	625
Bhilai	4	6	32	35	77	152	229
Total	69	107	893	500	1569	4183	5752

Financial Achievement of Telecom Factories for the year 1997-98.

(Figures in Crores)

Sl. No.	Telecom Factory	Target 1997-98	Turnover 1997-98
i.	Mumbai	45.00	41.00
ii.	Calcutta	56.00	64.60
iii.	Kharagpur	4.00	2.86
iv.	Wright Town (Jabalpur)	55.00	47.08
v.	Richhai (Jabalpur)	27.00	21.19
vi.	Bhilai	11.00	11.76
Total		198.00	188.49

Physical Performance: Achievement in respect of important items is as indicated below:

SL.No.	Items	Achievements 1997-98
(1) Telecom factory, Mumbai		
i.	C.D.Cabinets of Sorts	8525
ii.	C.T. Box 100 Pairs	61670
iii.	D.P.Boxes 10/20 Pairs	136400
iv.	Line Jack Unit	770000
v	Pay Phones	3240
vi.	MIDFs	1635
vii.	Modems	450
(2)	Telecom factory, Calcutta and Gopalpur	
i.	D.P. Boxes of sorts	96050
ii.	C.T. Box 100 pairs	70668
iii.	15 M Masts	4918
iv	Bkt.Ch. Iron 4 Wire	832500
v	Microwave Towers	1362
vi.	Buttenski Telephone	8225

vii.	MDF of Sorts	1783
viii.	Stalks of Sorts	370000
ix.	C.D.Cabinets of Sorts	3179
x.	U-Back	1116500
xi.	Line Jack Unit	700890
xii.	CBT - 80	2039
xiii.	Support Bracket	267000
(3)	Telecom factory, Khagarpur	
i.	Socket'B	32083
ii.	Saddles	815000
iii.	Sole Plate	124000
(4)	Telecom factory (wright town), (Jabalpur)	
i.	Tubes B-8 Equv. (Rivetted)	310260
ii.	C.D. Cabinets of Sorts	3563
iii.	Stalks of Sorts	378000
iv.	Bkt. Ch. Iron 4 Wire	469000
v.	Microwave Towers	2837 M.Tons
vi.	Line Jack Unit	336400
vii.	U-Back464000	
viii.	Masts 15 M	958 nos.
ix.	Masts 40 M	101
x.	Support Bracket	183750
(5)	Telecom factory- Richhai, Jabalpur	
i.	Tubes B-8 Equivalent (Welded)	336530
(6)	Telcom factory, Bhilai	
i.	Microwave Towers	3025 M Tones
ii.	15 M Masts	705 Nos.

Role of telecom factories

As in-house production units, Telecom factories are a source of uninterrupted supply and can be depended upon for extra supplies in the event of shortfall in supply from private sources apart from ensuring fair price in respect of certain items being supplied both by Telecom factories and the private manufacturers. Telecom factories have adapted modern production processes to achieve quality production and cost reduction so as to stand in competition with private companies. Product diversification is given due emphasis to utilise the available infrastructure and manpower. Factories have now entered new areas like Repair of cards, Telephone Instruments, Computers etc.

Following new items have been productionised during 1997-98:

i. CBT-95

ii. Support Bracket

iii. **TTH Towers**

Telecom quality assurance

The Telecom Quality Assurance Organisation of the Department of Telecommunications was formed in 1979 as a part of Technical and Development Circle but later became as an independent Telecom Quality Assurance Circle in 1986. Telecom Quality Assurance Circle has been one of the most vital Organisations covering all aspects of Quality-Assurance work thereby enabling standardisation and uniformity of approach and procedures. It is entrusted with the responsibility of assuring quality on a wide range of products and equipments inducted into Telecom network. To carry out the above work, the Telecom Quality Assurance Circle with Headquarters at Bangalore, functions with 84 Quality Assurance Centres located all over India and two Apex Laboratories namely, the Telecom Testing Laboratory (TTL) and Component Approval Centre for

Telecom (CACT). The TTL has also three branches at New Delhi, Hyderabad and Calcutta.

Activities

(i) Value of stores accepted during 1997-98 is Rs. 55,326 Millions.

(ii) One new QA Centres opened at Hyderabad (M/s. XL Telecom Ltd., Mallapur, Hyderabad-74).

(iii) 148 Infrastructure Assessments carried out for conventional products and 140 for TEC products.

(iv) 528 Type Approval Certificates issued.

(v) 11 nos. of Major Quality problems identified based on QA testing/Field feedback.

(vi) Approved Inspection Scheme introduced for 6 products.

(vii) Delegated Inspection Scheme introduced for 8 products.

(viii) First Product Qualification testing completed for 163 products.

(ix) 52 Telecom products taken up for Maintenance Approval.

(x) No. Important Meetings held - 21 and No. of Meetings where Senior QA Officers participated - 35.

(xi) 4 Documents issued during the year as Quality Manuals on various Telecom Products.

(xii) Rs. 1080.95 Lakh of Non-plan and Rs. 64.81 Lakh of Plan expenditure incurred during the year.

New facilities added in TTL/CACT

— Profile Projector has been procured and installed for inspection of PCBs.

— Tensile test machine of OFC Lab has been installed.

— Columns of High Performance Liquid Chromatography System have been added.

— Test programme has been done for testing 59 new components.

— Maintenance free battery for 3 KVA UPS System has been received to install at FA lab. of CACT

— Flash point and drop point tester for testing PHF/OF Cables Jellies has been installed in FA Lab. of CACT.

Activities of CACT

— 24,333 Components tested as part of Surveillance/Approval/FA activities.

— 477 Component Approvals issued.

— 14 Component Manufactures infrastructure Assessed.

— 27,995 Chamber hours utilised for climatic and environmental tests.

— 240 components were subjected to failure analysis.

— 45 reports generated by SCRAM.

— 82 Source Approval Certificate for raw material issued.

— 630 Nos. of Components/Equipments subjected to environmental tests.

UNDP project

Six Numbers of ITU-UNDP seminars were conducted at CACT, Bangalore with the help of foreign experts.

Seminars and meetings

QA Circle participated in 5 Seminars/Training programmes conducted by outside agencies. Training programmes on Quality and Reliability matters conducted by Telecom QA Circle, for the benefit of its personnel.

World telecom day

World Telecommunications Day was celebrated on 17th May, 1997. The CACT Laboratories were kept open for School/College students.

Personnel

Staff employment

The total number of staff employed and their distribution in different services is indicated in Table 14 of the Report. The total staff employed at the end of the year was 4.25 lakhs as compared to 4.29 lakhs during the last year. This includes staff in MTNL and industrial workers in the telecommunication factories also.

Scheduled castes and scheduled tribes

There were 74639 Scheduled Castes and 19920 Scheduled Tribes employees in the Department as on 31.3.1998. This includes 1579 sweepers.

Women employees

At the end of the year there were 53783 women employees out of total of 4.25 lakh employees in the Department.

Human resource development- training

Keeping in view rapid technological innovations and changes in the Telecom Sector, training programmes are organised so as to continuously upgrade and update the knowledge and skills of the telecom personnel. The strategy adopted by the Department in this direction comprises

(i) Strengthening and modernizing the training infrastructure.

(ii) Evolving appropriate training methodology for various cadres.

(iii) Deputing personnel for training to institutions in developed countries to acquire knowledge and expertise in latest technologies in Telecom field.

Training infrastructure

Presently the Department has 44 Telecom Training Centres comprising two apex level training centres namely, ALTTC, Ghaziabad and BRBRAITT, Jabalpur for training of telecom professionals and engineers, 15 Regional Telecom Training Centres (RTTCs) located at different regions in the country to provide training to supervisory staff of the Department and 27 CTTCs/DTTCs to cater to the training needs of field personnel.

In addition to above, temporary branch Telecom Training Centres in various circles were continued wherever necessary to expedite the training of staff in Restructured Cadres.

The training equipment at various training centres is upgraded continuously to keep pace with changing technology. Video Conferencing facility was also provided between BRBRAITT Jabalpur and TEC New Delhi during 1997-98.

Personnel trained

A total of 69,084 personnel were trained in various training centres during the year 1997- 98. This includes 144 foreigners trained in ALTTC, Ghaziabad and BRBRAITT Jabalpur. The details are given in Table 16. 67 Officers of the Department were deputed abroad during 1997-98 for training in modem switching, transmission technologies and management. 52 Officers of the Department were deputed for seminars and courses conducted by other departments and outside agencies.

Training under restructure scheme

Training for restructured cadres of Phone Mechanic, Telecom Technical Assistant (TTA) and Senior Telecom Operating Assistants is in progress. A total of 29531 Phone Mechanics, 4106 TTAs and 11224 Sr. TOAs were trained during the year 1997-98.

Training development activities

A UNDP Project in the area of Quality-Assurance to enhance Quality-Assurance capabilities of the Department of Telecom has just been completed. The project was widely appreciated by agencies including UNDP & ITU and above all by the manufacturers of Telecom components who have attained better confidence in production of Telecom components with much better quality.

A UNDP Project in the area of HRD & Management, which was launched in November-1 996, picked up momentum during the current financial year 1997-98 wherein the following achievements were made:-

(i) Officers deputed for Study Tour and Fellowships= 30

(ii) Experts/Consultants including CTA arrived in India = 15.5 manmonths

(iii) Equipment procured for ALTTC = Protocol analyser

Progress of special sub-plan

Tribal sub-plan

The Department has formulated Tribal Sub- Plan (TSP) as a part of the 9th Five Year Plan for providing telecom facilities in the tribal areas. For all round and faster development of Telecom facilities in tribal areas, the Department is treating these areas as special focus areas. The main objectives of the tribal sub-plan are:-

(i) To provide the telephone facility practically on demand in tribal areas by end of 9th plan.

(ii) To provide NSD facility to all exchanges in Tribal areas by end of 9th plan.

(iii) To provide public telephones in all tribal villages by the end of 9th plan.

Financial outlay and actual expenditure

The approved plan outlay for TSP for 1997-98 was Rs. 591.15 Crores (R.E.). The actual expenditure during 1997-98 was Rs. 468.74 Crores.

Physical targets and achievements

Statement showing the Physical Targets and Achievements during 1997-98 and Targets for 1998-99 are given in Table 12 of the Statistical Supplement.

Special component plan for the development of north eastern region

The Department of Telecom is giving special attention to the rapid development of telecom facilities in the NE Region of the country. During 1997-98 there was net addition of 78,614 lines of Telephone switching capacity, 59507 direct exchange lines and 2977 village public telephones. As on 31.3.98, all the 7 North Eastern States namely Arunachal Pradesh, Manipur, Meghalaya, Mizoram, Nagaland, Tripura and Assam had 100% electronic telephone exchanges. During 1998-99, 113200 lines of net switching capacity, 82000 direct exchange lines and 3900 village public telephones are planned to be provided in the North Eastern region.

National capital region (NCR)

In order to decongest the National Capital and to reduce the population pressure on it, National Capital Region consisting of 20 priority towns and 5 counter magnet towns spreading to 5 States surrounding the National Capital is getting special attention for development of infrastructure facilities including the telecom facilities in these towns. During 1997-98 Department of Telecom has provided 75656 lines of Telephone switching capacity and 83430 direct exchange lines in the Region.

During the 9th Plan period, all efforts will be made to improve the telecom facilities of NCR and to introduce various value added services to make it at par with Delhi, which is one of the demands of the NCR Planning Board. Also, it is aimed to make the telephone available on demand at the earliest during the 9th Plan period in the entire NCR region.

Use of Hindi

During the period under report O.L. Branch followed Rules & Regulations prescribed by the Department of Official Language. The main activities of the O.L. Branch were as given below:-

(i) Acquainted all the Telecom Circles/Administrative Off ices/Undertakings with the O.L. Act, Rules and instructions issued thereunder for their compliance for achieving the targets fixed by O.L. Department in their Annual Programme for the year under report.

(ii) Reviewed the Quarterly Progress Report regarding progressive use of Hindi received from all the Sections of DOT (Hq.) and all the Telecom Circles/ other Admn. Offices/Undertakings etc. and took necessary corrective measures in respect of those wherein defects were noticed.

(iii) Provided Hindi information through Hindi Vishesh Seva (177) and monitored thereof. Now this service has been extended by the Department in 30 cities.

(iv) Arranged nomination for Hindi training for those Officers/Officials who had not acquired working knowledge of Hindi. Similarly, Stenographers/

Typist who had not undergone training in Hindi Stenography/Typing were nominated for the above respective training courses.

(v) Carried out inspections of Telecom Circles/Admn. Offices/Undertakings to ensure as to what extent the provisions of O.L. Act/Rules and instructions issued thereunder were strictly adhered to. About 6 inspections were carried out during the year under review.

(vi) As usual Hindi Day/Week/Fortnight was organised from 1.9.97 to 15.9.97 which is a regular activity of every year prescribed by Deptt. of Official Language.

(vii) An Akhil Bhartiya Rajbhasha Sammelane was organised in D.O.T (HO) on 7th November 1997.

(viii) O.L. Branch works as a Co-ordinator from DOT (Hq.) during the course of inspections of Circles etc. by Committees of Parliament on Official Language which is also a regular feature every year. About 12 inspections were carried out by Committee of Parliament on Official Language during 97-98. Parliamentary Committee also inspected D.O.T (HQ) during the year under report.

(ix) Translated all the documents in Hindi/English specified in Section 3(3) of Official Language Act 1963 and Official Language Rule 1976, all the papers/reports to be laid by DOT on the table in both the Houses of Parliament.

(x) Four quarterly meetings of the Department Official Language Implementation Committee were held during the period under review.

(xi) A Hindi workshop for five days was conducted in D.O.T (HQ) to remove hesitation of officials in doing their daily official work in Hindi.

Welfare and sports activities

An amount of Rs. 4.75 crore has been provided for the Welfare & Sports activities to the Department of Telecommunications during the year 1997-98. An amount of Rs. 4,46,20,771/- has been disbursed to different Circles/U nits for meeting their Welfare& Sports expenditure from April '97 to March '98.

The following important schemes for grant of financial assistance from Welfare fund to the Telecom employees or their dependent have been formulated and are being enjoyed by our employees and their dependent as the case may be.

a) Financial assistance to the dependent of deceased employees.

b) Supply of sewing machines to the families of deceased employees.

c) Financial assistance in cases of death of casual labourers (temporary status mazdoor); in case of death of retired employees; in prolonged illness cases of employees; in serious illness/magi operations etc.; on account of prolonged illness of the dependent of employees; for nutritive diet for TB patients; by way of loans in emergency cases; to victims of natural calamities; handicapped for purchase of artificial limbs; to handicapped children on account of transport/ hostel mess charges; towards railway fares from headquarters to artificial limb centre.

d) Scholarships and awards.

e) Book awards and incentives to meritorious children.

f) Grant-in-aid to Recreation/Sports club.

g) Holiday excursion trips.

There is a Telecom. Women's Central Organisation (TWCO) for undertaking Welfare activities for Telecom women and their children which includes opening of creches, tailoring centres, nurs(schools and arts and crafts classes.

The annual grant to TWCO is Rs. 2 lakhs (and for its branch located in circles is Rs. 15,000/-). Creches can now be opened in both office buildings or in Colonies depending upon the consensus and convenience of the user employees. In any case, building would not be rented specifically for this purpose.

Out of 33 holiday homes at present functioning in important hill stations/health resorts, 14 are under administrative control of Department of Telecom. These are utilised by employees of Department for holidaying purpose.

To develop sports among Sportsmen, tournaments in 17 disciplines are conducted at differ places during 1997-98 on all-India basis. An amount of Rs. 66,69,721/- was spent for Sports Cultural activities during 1997-98.

P & T Sports Control Board has sent combined P&T team for National in the Power Lifting Weight lifting, Chess, Wrestling, and Kabaddi tournaments.

Work study

15 norms studies and 11 work measurements studies were completed during the year 1997-98 i.e. from 1.4.97 to 31.3.98.

Industrial assistance and export promotion group

The Industrial Assistance and Export Promotion Group of Production Wing of DOT is responsible for the development and regulation of the Telecom Industry in the country. The main activities of the Group are:

i. Providing assistance in formulation of Import and Export policies for the Telecom Sector.

ii. Providing assistance in formulation of foreign investment policies and procedures for the Telecom Sector.

iii. Processing of applications for foreign investment and foreign technology in Telecom Sect

iv. Matters relating to promotion of Telecom Exports including sponsoring of trade delegation, of up of Indian pavilions in international Exhibitions and Organisation of Seminars etc.

v. Assistance in matters relating to Customs and Excise duties and other Direct and Indirect Taxes for the Telecom Sector.

vi. Assistance in matters relating to Trade and Industrial policies for the Telecom Sector.

vii. Assistance to various industrial units in the Telecom Sector for implementation of their projects.

Manufacture of telecom equipments

India is a major manufacturer of a wide variety of Telecom Equipments. The growth in Telecom equipments production in the country is as follows:

(Rupees in crores)

	1992-93	'93-94	'94-95	'95-96	'96-97	'97-98
Production	3985	5500	7000	7750	8300	9960

Export of telecom equipments and services

Vigorous efforts are being made to increase the exports of Telecom equipments and services. India has now been recognised as a key supplier of products and technologies for rural Telecom by international organisations viz. ITU etc.

Growth in Exports of Telecom Equipments and services is as follows:

(Rs. in Crores

	1992-93	'93-94	'94-95	'95-96	'96-97	'97-98
Service	282	456	598	1108	1458	2232
Consultancy	119	118	207	235	270	313
Hardware	24	58	131	310	240	296

Approval in respect to direct foreign investment (DFI).

An amount of Rs. 31466.11 Crore has been approved as Direct foreign investment from 1.8.91 to 31.8.98 in various Telecom manufacturing and services projects as per following details. The actual inflow during this period has been Rs. 3985.12 crores.

S. No.	Category (Rs in Crores)	No. of Approval	FDI Approvals
i.	Radio Paging Service	46	1166.39
ii.	Cellular/Basic Telecom Service	110	20724.59
iii.	Manufacturing and other Telecom Services	296	9575.13
	Total	452	31466.11

Private investment promotion cell

This group has recently been created to encourage, stimulate and facilitate private investment in telecom sector and to smoothen the implementation of these projects. Main activities of this group are:

Promotional Activities:

— Interaction with Business Councils/Industry Associations.

— Interaction with Indian Investment Centre and other

Government/Semi-Government bodies concerned with investment promotion.

— To recommend formation of policies to catalyse and stimulate private investment in Telecom Sector.

— Printing of Promotional Literature and their distribution.

— Organisation of investment Conferences/Seminars/ Exhibitions and dissemination of information, arrange publicity about avenues/scope of private investment in Telecom Sector.

— Deputation of officers from DoT for attending the National/International Conferences/Seminars/ Exhibitions concerned with investment promotion.

Training

During the year, as many as 441 Officers of various levels have been trained in vigilance functions.

Other activities

Special CBI Cells:- Special CBI Cells set up in metro cities to prevent leakage of telecom revenue continued to perform well and give encouraging results. Though it is not possible to quantify their gains in concrete financial terms, these Cells had registered 120 cases involving 130 Departmental officials and 33 outsiders.

Special Squads:- Special Squads were formed in the year 1995 for surprise visits to the subscriber's premises and Telephone Exchanges. The main job of these squads is random checking of equipments, telephone lines etc. to find out tempering, if any, with the equipments or lines in the Switch Room/external plant. Follow-up action was taken on various irregularities/omissions found by the special squads. This has resulted in considerable improvement in the services and preventing misuse of lines.

Technical Solutions:- A committee was set up in May, 1995 to study the technical and administrative aspects of revenue leakage. The Committee submitted its report in July, 1995. Several recommendations of the Committee on use of sensitive commands, carrying out of software modifications to stop misuse of certain commands for stoppage of metering etc. were implemented. Another committee was setup under the Chairmanship of Sr. DDG (Vig) in Dec., 1996 for carrying out detailed study on technical and administrative aspects to prevent revenue leakage. The Committee has submitted its report and its recommendations are under implementation by the field units.

Management information system (MIS)

MIS Cell helps in monitoring the performance of Telecom Circles, Metro Districts, MTNL & Mtce. Regions through various MIS Reports. The following Monthly statements are submitted to the Telecom Commission.

— Top management report.

— Status Report of Equipped Capacity, DELs and Waiting List of Telecom Circles/Metro Distts./MTNL in respect of Telephones.

— Achievement Report in respect of net increase in Telephone Equipped Capacity and DELs against the target fixed in respect of Telecom Circles/Metro Distts./MTNL.

— Special Monthly MIS Report.

(a) Service performance of Telecom Circles/Metro Distts./MTNL.

(b) Development activities on all-India basis.

(c) Financial Performance of Department on all-India basis along with Collection Efficiency circle-wise.

(d) Position of supplies from suppliers in respect of equipments for Department against the target of supplies for the month.

MIS publication on Telecom Network, Telecom Development & Financial Performance and other statistical information for each financial year is published every year. It contains information about performance of all the Telecom Circles, Metro Districts, MTNL and Telecom Maintenance Regions along with the information about Volume & Growth of various services provided by Department. The data compilation work for the publication of MIS book for the year 1997-98 is in final stage.

Economic Research Unit (ERU) and Statistics (STT) Section

The following studies/exercises were completed during 1997-98:

(i) Call Slab Wise Distribution Pattern of Subscribe rs/ Calls - A case study of 8/28 Telecom Districts : 1993-94 and 1994-95.

(ii) Impact of Tariff revision effective from 1.5.93 on subscribers calling pattern and revenue.

(iii) Telephone Demand Projections - Towns having exchanges with 200 lines and above 1997-2007.

(iv) Telephone Revenue - An analysis of Trends and An Examination of Determinants for 1993-94 and 1994-95.

(v) Examination of "Federal Communications Commission (FCC)" Document - Notice of Proposed Rule making (NPRM) - from economic angle.

(vi) Two Decades of studies in Telecom Economics.

(vii) Committee on "Metered Calls and Revenue per DEL per day".

International co-operation/seminars/meetings

Bilateral Co-operation Meetings

i) Joint Working Group/Joint Working Commission & Inter-Ministerial meetings.

ii) 26 Bilateral Co-operation meetings held in various Ministries from 1st April '97 to 31st March '98. 12.9.1.2. Delegation (Dignitories from Foreign Countries)

(A) 9 delegations have visited DOT, as mentioned below:

i) H. E. Mr. Mimoun Aoujil, Secretary General of the Ministry of Posts & Telecom, Morocco.

ii) Mr. Pitak Intrawideyanunt, Dy. Foreign Minister of Thailand.

iii) H.E. Mr. Wolfgang Boetsch, Minister of Posts and Telecommunications, Federal Republic of Germany along with a large German Government business delegation.

iv) H. E. Mr. Alyaksandr Lukashenka, President of Belarus.

v) Mr. V.Goncharenko, Minister of Communication of Belarus.

vi) Mr. Reed Hunt, Chairman, US Federal Communications Commission (FCC) and Chief Regulator of the Telecom Industry in the United States, along with his delegation team, has called on the Hon'ble Minister of Communications on 26th June 1997 & Chairman TC on 27th June '97 in Sanchar Bhawan, New Delhi.

vii) Mr. Vonya Mccann US Co-ordinator for International Communication& Information policy, along with a large American delegation of FCC officials and businessmen.

viii) Mr. William Daley, United States Commerce Secretary along with a large delegation of American businessmen.

ix) H. E. Dr. Peter Medgyessy, Finance Minister of the Republic of Hungary.

x) Ms. Rita Murrell, and Mr. Ashok Pasricha, Engineer from the U.S. Export-import Bank (EXIM) called on DDG(IR) to meet with EXIM Borrowers, guarantors and appropriate Government entities in India to discuss pending and potential business.

xi) Mr. David Brar of Agriteam Canada and Mr. Shabir Ahmad of JPs Associates called on DDG(IR) to discuss CIDA:s project, (a) establishment of radio advisory council and (b) Consumer watchdog facility regarding telecom services.

(B) MOU Signed:-

i) A Memorandum of Understanding was signed between Government of India & Germany in the field of Posts & Telecommunications in DOT Sanchar Bhawan at Ministerial level on 2.9.97.

ii) n agreement was signed between Government of India & Belarus in the field of Posts & Telecommunications in Vigyan Bhawan at Ministerial level on 27.9.97.

iii) A Memorandum of Understanding on Mutual Cooperation on Telecommunications between Deptt. of Telecom India and the Ministry of Industry, France was signed at Secretary level on 21.1.98 in Paris.

Seminars/workshops/meetings/training - national level

i) 35 DOT Officers participated in Seminar/Meetings etc. held in India organised by various International Organisations.

ii) Procured cases regarding grant of permission to foreign Telecom Companies for establishing their branch offices in India.

Exhibitions (international & National):-

(A) International:-

i) "Asia Telecom '97" in Singapore from 9-14 June, 1997. Department of Telecommunications participated along with its associated Public Sector Undertakings and private companies.

ii) Industrial and Technological Exhibition of India at Beijing (China), from 7-11 July '1997. C-DOT & TCIL participated in the exhibition. A delegation led by Chairman (TC) also visited the exhibition.

iii) "Telecom Expo '90" at Hanoi (Vietnam) from 2-6 December 1997: Department of Telecommunications participated along with Public Sector Undertakings such as C-DOT, ITI, and TCIL.

iv) "The Pride of India" Exhibition from 14-17 January, 1998 in Hanoi (Vietnam): Public Sector Undertakings of the Department of Telecommunications, ITI, HTL and C-DOT participated. The event was to commemorate 50 years of India's Independence.

v) An "Indian Trade Exhibition" was organised at World Trade Centre, Mexico City (Mexico), from 3-9 March '98.

vi) "Cebit '98" at Hanover (Germany) from 9-25 March, 1998.

(B) National/regional:-

i) Gateway '97 at Science City Calcutta, from 5-9 November 1997.

ii) Sishu Utsav '97 at Durgapur, West Bengal from 11 -25 November 1997.

iii) India International Trade Fair '97 was held at Pragati Maidan, New Delhi from 14-27 November 1997 DoT pavilion was inaugurated by Hon'ble Minister of Communications.

iv) COMMS India '97 from 9-11 December 1997 at Pragati Maidan, New Delhi.

v) 11th Industrial India Trade Fair at Calcutta 19-31 December 1997.

vi) All India Agriculture, Science and Industrial Trade Fair '98 at Kalyani, Nadia (West Bengal) from 1st to 15th January, 1998. It was organised by Jai Prakash Narayan Janmotsav Committee.

vii) "Sunderban Mela '98" at Canning Town, West Bengal, from 3rd to 12th January, 1998. It was organised by Bandhu Mahal.

Deputation of officers to foreign countries from 1st April '97 to 31st March 1998 is as follows:-

i) Deputation of 31 officers to Geneva, Singapore Cascais (Portugal), Manila, Tornoto & Seoul for different study groups of ITU-T/ITU-R/ITU-D.

ii) Deputation of 16 officers to Shanghai (China), Kathmandu, Tokyo, Bangkok, & Chaingmai (Thailand) for attending APT Meetings/Seminars.

iii) Deputation of 18 officers to Phuket (Thailand), Bangkok, Singapore, Geneva and Kathmandu for attending Meetings/Workshop/TCDC, Consultancies with UNDP/ITU Project.

iv) Deputation of 36 officers for attending miscellaneous International Meetings/Seminars/Conferences to Germany, USA, Seoul, London, Chicago, Copen hengon (Denmark) and Auckland.

v) A high level business delegation led by Sh.

R.N.Bhardwaj, DDG(IR), accompanied by Sr. officers of the level of Executive Directors from I.TI., C-DOT, & TCIL visited Hanoi (Vietnam) from 28-31st July, 1997, to explore the possibilities of business in Telecommunications.

vi) Indian delegation participated in Asia Pacific Telecommunity (APT) Regional meeting for WRC-97 organised by APT from 28th July to 1st August '97 at Seoul, Republic of Korea.

vii) Hon'ble MOC inaugurated the Conference of India Industry in association with US Trade and Development Agency & U.S. Department of Commerce.

viii) A four member DoT delegation headed by the Chairman, Telecom Commission visited France from 19th to 21st January 1998 to participate in the meeting of Indo-French Joint Committee on Posts and Telecommunications.

ix) A three member DoT Delegation headed by the Chairman, Telecom Commission visited Canada from 2nd to 6th February 1998 in connection with CIDA proposals in the session of Telecommunications.

x) A satellite Coordination meeting was held between Administrations of USA and India, during 9-13 February 1998 for Coordination of PANAMSAT and INSAT Satellite networks.

xi) Indo-Ethiopia Joint Trade Committee meeting was held on 25-26th February, 1998 in Addis Ababa. Sr. representatives from C-DoT, HTL and R&D attended the meeting.

— About 55 foreign delegates and 200 officers from DOT & other PSU's (TCHQ, C-DOT MTNL, TCIL, ITI, HTL, & TEC etc.) participated in "Asia-Pacific

Telecom Trade & Finance Colloquium" held in Vigyan Bhawan, New Delhi from 3-5 Nov. 1997. Hon'ble MOS(C) has inaugurated this event on 3.11.97.

— "A National Telecom Seminar' was held on 14th Jan. '98 in Hotel Ashok, Chanakya Puri, New Delhi to celebrate "50th year of our Independence." The seminar was inaugurated by Chairman Telecom Commission. Dy. Secretary General (ITU)), Geneva, Mr. Henry Chasia delivered a keynote address on the occasion.

Network division

Meeting held

(i) DSLCC: meeting was held with the representatives of Defence authorities and Deptt. of Telecom on 4-4-97 at Sena Bhawan, New Delhi.

(ii) Joint Study group meeting with officers of Defence authorities and Deptt. of Telecom were held on 23-9-97 and 10-11 -97 in Sena Bhawan.

(iii) Steering Committee meeting between representatives of Defence and Dir (NW), DOT was held on 19-8-97 in South Block, New Delhi.

Miscellaneous activities

(a) ATNs & Audit paras

(i) 17 ATNs have been vetted and cleared by Audit.

(ii) For one ATN of 95-96, the cell is vigorously taking up the case with CGMT (MHR) for want of detailed particulars of dues.

(b) Territorial army cases

(i) Additional benefits viz Best training Award among TA Trainees and introduction of TA medals among

TA Personnel are under process of sanction. The case has not yet been finalised by Finance.

(ii) Case of splitting of Annual Trg. Camp for TA personnel is under process.

(iii) Out of 14 proposed TA personnel, 7 have been trained in Satellite communication through NW cell. For the remaining personnel Trg. programme has been scheduled in this year.

(c) War-contingent circuit

Feasibility reports of War contingent circuits from pending units are being updated. Some more information has been received from different units.

(d) Army HQRS

Sanction of 13 STD, PCOs for the Border area of J&K has been obtained from MOD up to 28th Feb. '98. The case for extension up to 28-2-99 has already been processed.

Civil wing

The Civil Wing in the Department of Telecom came into existence in the year 1963. It is responsible for executing and maintaining the Buildings and services infrastructure for the Department. Its activities include planning and execution of:-

i) Technical Buildings for housing Telecom Equipment.

ii) Administrative Offices.

iii) Staff Quarters.

iv) Cable Ducts.

v) Civil Works for Transmission Towers.

vi) Air Conditioning.

vii) Substations Engine Alternator.

viii) Services such as Fire Fighting and Environmental Works.

It is also responsible for maintenance, rehabilitation and retrofitting of Building assets.

Work load

The activities of the Civil Wing have increased many folds over the years. The workload of the Civil Wing has progressively increased from a mere Rs. 4 crores in the year 1963 to Rs. 1,000 crores in the current financial year. In order to cater for the stringent requirement of high technology telecom equipment, the Civil wing is constantly upgrading the technology of designs, construction, air conditioning and other systems installed in the Buildings.

Organisational setup

The Civil Wing has three disciplines viz. Civil, Electrical and Architecture. All these three disciplines provide inputs for planning and construction of a Building Project. Each discipline is headed by a Sr. DDG in the headquarters reporting to Member (Production). The field set up is headed by Chief Engineers/Chief Architects located at various places.

Achievements

The physical achievements of the Civil Wing during the period 1997-98 are as follows:-

Sl. No.	Type of Bldg. Completed During 1997-98	No. of Building
i)	MAX-I	62
ii)	MAX-II	500
iii)	CTO/DTO	10
iv)	Transmission Buildings	78

V)	Towers Foundation	257
vi)	Admn. Buildings	16
vii)	Staff Quarters	2486
viii)	Other Buildings	212
ix)	Cable duct (in route Kms.)	124.94

Staff

P&T Building Works Service - Group "A"

Gazetted

	Civil	Electrical	Architecture	Total
Higher Admn. Grade	1	1	1	3
Senior Administrative Grade	20	9	4	33
Junior Administrative Grade	105	36	16	157
Senior Time Scale	250	97	38	385
Junior Time Scale	49	11	25	85
Total	425	154	84	663

Telecom commission

Composition of Telecom commission

The composition of the full-time Members of the Telecom Commission during 1997-98 was as follows:-

Chairman	Sri A. V. Gokak	W. E. F.	4.11.96
Member (Finance)	Sri A. Prasad	W.E.F.	31.07.97
Member (Production)	Sri R.R.N.Prasad	W. E. F.	01.10.97
Member (Services)	Sri P. S. Saran	W.E.F.	11.01.95
Member (Technology)	Sri N. K. Sinha	W. E. F.	15.11.95

13

Future Prospects

With the number of telephones in India aggregating to a mere 5.8 million to service a population of over 850 million people, telecommunications is an industry of tremendous growth potential. It is also one of the most profitable business areas in India today with the pay back on a line being only two years.

The new Ministry of Communication has drawn up a very ambitious 26 point program for this Industry. Some of the highlights are that private participation has been invited for building and operation of telecom networks in 'growth centres and satellite towns'.

In the new Industrial Policy, telecom equipment was delicenced and thrown open to foreign investment. Several joint ventures came up- GPI and K.K. Birla, Ericcson with their long term collaborators the Jiwarajkars, AT&T with Tata Telecom, Fujitsu with the Punjab State Electronic Production and Development Corporation and Alcatel with B.K. Modi. Of these companies gearing up to meet the indigenous requirements, the last two are near ready to commence production of equipment to meet the specifications set out by the Department of Telecommunications.

The Ministry of Communication has in October this year allowed eight private companies to establish cellular telephone systems in the four metropolitan cities kof Delhi, Bombay, Calcutta and Madras. In each of the four metros, the two private companies would operate the system along with their two foreign partners. Tenders are expected to be floated soon inviting private manufacturers to set up value-added celluler telephone systems in other secondary cities in the country. Mobile telephones will be made available against foreign exchange payment. Video conferencing, Email, Radio Paging and other value added services and manufacturing of ten thousand line exchanges, will be available to joint/private sector without licensing (capacity) regulation.

Until now only terminal equipment and PABX manufacturing was permitted in private sector subject to lecensing.

New Import Export Policy

A new Import-Export Policy was announced on 1st April, 1992. The policy statement eliminated a number of import categories, exceptions and exemptions, special lists, open lists etc. The new 5 year exim policy makes trade "free" subject to a small negative list. Even the short negative list which prohibits import of certain items is likely to be curtailed further during the year.

The Finance Minister, Dr. Manmohan Singh, while inaugurating the International Asia Pacific Conference on private sector has stated that "bureaucratic controls would be fully dismantled, quantitative import restrictions phased out and customs tariff reduced to international levels to make the private sector vibrant."

Collaboration by non-Small Scale Industrial units for items reserved for the SSI sector is allowed subject to the condition that the firms concerned would undertake to export at least 75% of its output. Applications for 100% EOUs are cleared by the SIA and those for 100% Export Processing Zone (EPZ) units are cleared by the

Development Commissioner of the particular EPZ, subject to the guidelines aplicable to such units.

Export obligations are no longer imposed in other cases of collaboration. Instead, the export offers made by the applicants are taken note of as being in the nature of a gentlemen's agreement, and are not linked to legal or bank guarantees. Their fulfilment is a matter of trust, and not compulsion.

The Government has liberalised the guidelines for * automatic approval in 30 days for all cases involving an equity of upto US $ two million.

The Government has initiated steps to deregulate the domestic civil aviation industry and bring an end to the public sector monopoly in domestic civil aviation. The Ministry of Civil Aviation has proposed to withdraw the three major constraints on private taxi operators namely:

- Restriction on level of fare.
- Route restriction.
- Flight time restriction.

The ministry has given support to the 'open sky policy' for air taxi licenses in India. Selling Indian airlines or Air India is however not on the immediate agenda.

Liberalisation and 'open sky policy' has opened the vast domestic market to new scheduled airlines in India. There are 22 registered private airlines of which a few are already operational. The most notable being East West Airlines which has already acquired 3% of the total domestic market, that was till now monopolised by Indian Airlines.

The ministry of Civil Aviation and Tourism has recently invited foreign capital and technology for 'collaborative partnership' for an "integrated development of the Indian aviation industry".

'Liberalisation window to opportunities was the theme of the 41st annual convention of the Travel Agents' Association of Inida, held at Hydrabad recently.

Many interesting facts emerged during the convention. Partial convertibility has made visiting India and even shopping an inexpensive proposition. For example, there is a charactered flight every day from Uzbekistan carrying 240 passengers stopping at New Delhi for a day of shopping!

In a radical departure form the Industrial Policy of 1956, the Union Government has announced that it will allow 100% foreign equity participation for setting up of power plants in India. It has also permitted substantial modification in the Electricity (Supply) Act 1948 to hasten the private sector's participation in the ailing power sector.

These two decisions have been taken by the cabinet and the bill containing the amendments in the Electricity (Supply) Act and the 100% foreign equity participation proposals will be tabled soon before the Parliament.

The 100% foreign equity participation proposals allows free repatriation of profits and other incentives. Besides, it will facilitate foreign parties to set up power plants without time delays, which are solely responsible for the cost escalation in the power projects.

Proposals from foreign investors for new power units are expected to be cleared through a high powered committee. The domestic private company's proposals will be cleared through a single window to minimise bureaucratic and other delays. The Government is likely to invite various foreign consortia including non-resident Indians (NRI's), particularly those in Japan and the UK to come forward.

Since the 1960's, the two public sector companies, Oil & Natural Gas Commission (ONGC) and Oil India Limited have held a monopoly over oil exploration in India. ONGC is seeking a change of its status to an autonomous corporation with the freedom to raise its resources directly from markets in India and overseas. It is prepared to enter into new projects such as country wide gas grid in collaboration with the private sector. It is understood that 73 drilling and exploratory blocks have been offered to international oil companies through international tendering. The Government has invited offers for joint ventures to develop designated medium-sized as also small sized oil and gas fields offering a range of incentives. Companies may singly or as a consortium bid by the 31st December 1992. Major tax concessions are made both for Indian and foreign companies engaged in oil exploitation. Income Tax will be levied at a flat rate of 50% without surcharge as against 65% now applicable to foreign companies in other businesses.

The Government has accorded status of importance to the Bombay High oil producing belt in the Arabian Sea and initiated highly sophisticated defence procedures for safeguarding the rigs from aggression.

Potential estimates claim that India should produce 70 metric tonnes of crude per annum by 1999 and will be considered a major economic power of the next century.

The rate of tax applicable to foreign companies continue to be 65%. Surcharge is not levied in the case of non-resident assessees.

Section 80 HHC of Income Tax Act 1961 provides for 100% exemption from income tax if the entire business income is generated from exports. The deductions available to an assessee involved in exports in now to be calculated on a new formula. The formula makes a distinction between a manufacturer exporter and a trading exporter. The actual deduction is calculated taking into consideration the FOB value of the exports as against the turnover and profits/gains of the business.

Under the provisions of Section 80-0, 50% of technical services fees, royalties etc derived under an approved agreement are deductible from income. This concession which was available to Indian corporate bodies has now been extended to non corporate bodies. This concession has been granted with the prupose of encouraging professionals such as architects, accountants etc to earn foreign exchange for the country. Further clarifications are expected from the Government on how this scheme would be applied to professionals as prior approval of agreements may be very difficult to administer.

Some immediate effects of the changes outlined above can be seen from the following events:

— As early as April 1992, a 1243% increase in foreign investment has been registered in India since the announcement of the liberalised industrial policy in July 1991.

— Foreign Collaborations in India recently approved by the Indian Government include companies like General Motors, General Electric, Coca Cola, Suzuki, Leasaffre (French), GERB (German), Buhler (Swiss), IBM, BMW, Ford etc. In the communication sector, AT&T, Siemens, France and British Telecom have shown keen interest in bidding for setting up cellular phone networks in India.

— 100 senior Japanese business executives spent a week in India in February 1992 and Nomura Securities Company has established a presence in

Delhi. The opening of a trading office of a securities house in known to be a major jumping off point for further investment in India.

— 200 foreign participants attended the Euromoney conference in Delhi on "Business, Finance and Investment in India" in the last week of March, 1992.

New Horizons

In the recent few months, with the Bombay Stock Market Scandal in which banks and financial institutions stand to lose upto Rs. 30 billion, inflation running upto 13% on occasions and other regional and national political problems, the feeling has been that the Government is now in the danger of letting opportunities slip away. The Government did announce de-licensing of the electronic industry, liberalisation which would permit foreign financial institutions to invest in India and permission to open branch offices by foreign companies in the last few months to counter the allegations that there has been a slow down in the economic reform process. Although there may be some truth in this allegation the process of liberalisation has certainly not stopped. The Government has given an assurance that it will endeavour to proceed with the intended further liberalisation as promised.

On the whole, along with devaluation of the rupee in June 1991, the new trade policy and the further reforms promised includding full convertibility of the rupee, if the new Industrial Policy and its effect does turn out to what it promises to be, new horizons will open. This should lead to faster growth of industries in India. Indian industries would be open and accessible to the world. The opening up of new areas such as air transportation and power generation for private sector participation will result in opportunities for contractors and financial institutions to bid for project and asset work. The feeling in India is that a clear signal has been sent to industrialists, both local and foreing, that the government really means business. The radical nature of the industrial policy has met and continues to meet some resistance from the bureaucratic machinery which it seeks to dismantle. Its fine print still requires further clarifications. But more important than the fine print is the inescapable fact the political power has finally recognised that it is time for a new order to emerge. For some, their efforts may have fallen short of expectations, but the Government has acted, at last.

This update has been prepared by Thakker & Thakker Solicitors & Advocates, Bombay, for the AIJA 1992 conference in Bombay on "Emerging Investment Opportunities in India". The Update is necessarily of general nature and seeks to provide information only on some of the major changes announced by the Government and cannot be regarded as legal advice.

Status of the Indian Telecom Network

India today operates one of the largest telecom networks in Asia comprising

— Over 20 172 telephone exchanges;

— About 118 400 route kms of coaxial terrestrial UHF/ microwave radio relay systems up to 140 Mbit/s apart from analogue systems;

— 23 300 kilometres of optical fibre systems comprising of systems up to 565Mb/s;

— 50 per cent of Transmission network is digitalised.

About 7 700 cities and towns are connected to the National Subscriber Dialling (NSD) network and the Department of Telecommunications (DOT) plans to extend the facility to all automatic exchanges by 1997.

Fully automatic International Subscriber Diallilng

(ISD) service is available to 237 countries through two international earth stations and submarine cable systems. Trunk manual service is also available to all countries.

To meet the low speed data communication needs of Business/industrial units in Remote and far flung areas, a Business. Message Network (RABMN) with a hub-station near Delhi, having a capacity of 1000 subscribers has been commissioned. About 456 Very Small Aperture Terminals (VSAT) are deployed in this network for providing data service at maximum speeds up to 9.6kbits.

A dedicated Packet Switched Public Data Network (PSPDN), with international access for computer communication services is available in the country with speeds up to 2Mbit/s.

For providing international connectivity, a Gateway Packet Switching System (GPSS), is available which offers the capability of sophisticated telecommunication networking terminals and computers internationally.

INSAT satellite systems are being used to provide over 4126 two-way speech circuits through 165 earth stations across the length and breadth of the country. In 1975, the government of India took a decision to have its system for meeting domestic communication needs of the country and approved the scheme in 1977 for the multi purpose Indian National Satellite System (INSAT).

The INSAT-I series of satellites, comprising four satellites were launched in 1982, 1983, 1988 and 1990 respectively. INSAT-II series of the satellites comprising four satellites in orbit and one ground spare, are being manufactured indigenously. Under this series, INSAT-IIA was launched in July 1992 and INSAT-IIB Satellite was launched in July 1993.

The present space segment comprises of * INSAT IIA

and IIB Satellites in orbit. The ground segment of INSAT-ID & INSAT-IIA, IIB comprises of 82 fixed Satellite earth stations. In addition to the above, 29 satellite earth stations have been commissioned as captive networks to meet the telecommunication needs of Government undertakings.

Besides above fixed satellite earth stations the ground segment also comprises 23 mobile terminals including three Flyaway Terminals. These terminals are capable of being transported to different parts of the country by road/air to restore the telecommunication services as well as to meet an urgent telecommunication need from any part of the country. There are also nine special routes/networks.

About 185000 villages out of 604 734 villages are provided with telecommunications facililties;

There were 2.5 telephones per 1000 population in the rural areas at the end of march 1995, as against the figure of 107 in the country as a whole. These figures are expected to become 3.00 and 15.00 respectively by the year 1997 as per the modest government investment. Private sector participation, which is expected shortly, will raise telephone density considerably.

The total equipped capacity of the Indian local network is 12 million with over 10 million main lines. There has been a rise of 25 per cent in telephone traffic in 1991-1992 and 35 per cent in 1992-1993 as compared to the previous year.

The pending demand however is 215 million and is growing at over 20 per cent per annum. In the past the registered demand has grown at a rate of 10 to 13 per cent per annum while the supply remained between 9 to 10.5 per cent. As a consequence the waiting list has grown. Over the last two years, we have stepped up the growth rate to 15 per cent per annum to see a slight dip in the demand.

The Indian Telecommuinications network provides nearly 400 000 Long Distance Switching Circuits with 94 per cent digitization.

A number of state-of-the-art switching technologies have been inducted in Indian network, ie FETEX 150, EWSD, AXE 10, No.5 ESS, OCB 283, System X, NEAX 61E and the indigenous CDoT.

Enhancement of capacity and digitalization of the transmission network is being carried out with optical fibre, digital microwaves and satellite.

A great emphasis is being laid on R&D of sophisticated digital switching and transmission equipment to meet india's urban and rural needs. The Centre for Development of Telematics (C-DoT) has successfully designed a family of digital-SPC switching systems from small to large main automatic exchanges.

Technology for several transmission products such as 10 channel UHF-600 MHz, 2/8 and 8/34 Digital mux, Satellite Based Rural Telegraph Network (SBRTN) Single Channel VHF and 2/8 Mbit/s OLTE has also been indigenously developed by CDoT and technology successfully transferred to a large number of local manufacturers. CDoT technology has also been offered to other countries as well.

Value added services are being indigenously developed exchanges through introduction of better signalling features such as Common Channel Signalling No. 7 and through ISDN.

The ultimate goal of R&D units is however to lead to the development of an Intergrated Services Digital Network (ISDN) and eventually to Broadband ISDN (B-

ISDN) through Synchronous Digital Hierachy (SDH). Digital Access Cross Connect System (DACCS), Asynchronous Transport Module (ATM) etc.

There is a Telecommunications Engineering Centre (TEC) for issuing of specifications, type approvals, interface approvals and evaluation of new telecom products and for standardisation.

Over the years, the Department of Telecom, have built up extensive training facilities starting at the apex with Advanced Level Telecommunications Training Centre, near Delhi, set up with the systems and support of the UNDP and ITU.

The Telecommunications Training Centre at Jabalpur and 11 Regional and 25 State and District Level Training Centres also provides extensive training facilities. India has been extending assistance to Asia and Pacific countries too in meeting their training needs in the high tech areas of telecommunications.

Through DOT's consultancy group known as Telecommunication Consultancy India Limited (TCIL), India has been offering a wide spectrum of consultancy services in the international arena.

These include technical and management support, training, inspection, rehabilitation, modernization of existing systems, techno-economic studies in the core sectors of engineering and design studies, besides construction management and electronic data processing etc.

The consultancy services, include feasibility studies, network design studies, software support, installation, testing and commissioning of switching systems and transmission systems, operation and maintenance of networks.

TCIL has executed various contracts abroad and has been operating in about 28 countries.

The Indian Telegraph (Amendment) Bill, 1995

The National Telecom Policy 1994, has inter-alia laid emphasis on achieving the universal service, bringing the quality of Telecom service to world standard, provision of the widest permissible range of services to meet the customer's demand at reasonable price and participation of the companies registered in India in the area of basic telecom services as also making arrangements for protection and promotion of consumers' interest and ensuring fair competition. The Department of Telecomomunications feel that to achieve these objectives, there is need to separate regulatory functions from service providing functions which will be in keeping with the prevailing general trend in the world. It has, therefore, proposed to set up an independent Telecom Regulatory Authority to be called 'Telecom Regulatory Authority of India' which, to begin with, will be non-statutory in character but will have well defined functions and responsibilities and powers to play the role of a watch-dog body for the Telecom sector in an effective manner.

The Indian Telegraph Act, 1885 regulates the functioning of Telecommunications services in the country. Under Section 4 of the Indian Telegraph Act, 1885, the Central Government has the exclusive right of establishing, maintaining and working telegraphs and under the first provision of this section, it may grant a licence on such conditions and in consideration of such payment as it thinks fit to any persons to establish, maintain or work a telegraph within any part of the country. Under Section 4(2) of the Act, the Central Government may by notification in the Official Gazette delegate to the Telegraph Authority all or any of its powers under the first proviso to subsection (1). Section 3(6) of the Indian Telegraph Act, 1885 describes Director General (Posts and Telegraphs) as the Telegraph Authority and includes any officer empowered by him to perform all or any of the functions of the Telegraph Authority under the Act. Presently, the Secretary, Department of Telecommunications who has been notified as the Director General Telecommunications in his capacity as a Telegraph Authority exercises regulatory powers and performs regulatory functions as delegated by the Central Government under the Indian Telegraph Act, 1885. In order to vest the powers of the Telegraph Authority with the proposed Regulatory Authority in respect of certain assigned functional areas. It has become necessary to amend Section 3(6) of the Indian Telegraph Act, 1885 by including "any statutory or non-statutory authority".

The secretary, Department of Telecommunications stated in evidence that at present all the regulatory authority under the Indian Telegraph Act is exercised by the Secretary, Department of Telecommunications. This power of the telegraph authority can be further delegated by him to another officer of the Government. It cannot be delegated to a statutory or a non-statutory authority as such. So, the basic purpose of the proposed amendment of Section3(6) of the Indian Telegraph Act, 1885 is to delegate certain regulatory powers of the Telegraph authority to the proposed Telecom Regulatory Authority.

The Secretary, Department of Telecommunications further clarified that the reasons for not coming up with a comprehensive Bill to setup a statutory with independent powers at this stage, are that the Government would like to watch the working of such an authority for a year or two and learn from such an experience. After getting the feed-back from the

Chairman and Members of the authority and various interest groups viz, operators and subscribers etc., it would frame a comprehensive law to make it a statutory authority. Then the authority will derive its powers directly from an Act of Parliament.

The witness further told the Committee that "the need for amendment is based not only on Government perceptions of the local market but also arises from the international experience that wherever there has been a situation of more than one player in the market scene, a need has been felt for an independent umpire. The current trend in the telecommunication sector the world-over is to distance policy making functions, operational functions and regulatory functions from each other and to entrust regulatory functions to an independent Regulatory Authority for regulating Telecom services".

The Secretary, Department of Telecommunications informed the Committee that in due course the proposed authority would be independent and autonomous; it would operate outside the Government, at arm's length from the Government so that it could inspire the confidence of various operators as well as the subscribers. He further added that for this purposes the intention of the Government is to ensure that it is manned by people of eminence and independent views. Therefore, the Cabinet has decided that it would be chaired by a retired or a serving Chief Justice of a High Court or a retired or a serving Judge of the Supreme Court and it will have two members who should have worked in the State Government or the Central Government in a position not lower than the position of an additional Secretary to Government of India for a period of three years. These Members would enjoy the status of Secretary to Govt. of India. It was further stated that the tenure of the Chairman and the Members would be secure and protected. Their removal will require the same safeguards as are available to Judges of the Supreme Court. Similarly their emoluments and other terms and conditions of service would not be changed to their disadvantage. The Secretary Department of Telecommunications stated that the apparent idea was to send across a strong signal that there would be an authority who would act independently, impartially, in an objective manner to protect the interests of the operators as also of the subscribers.

Clarifying the position further in reply to a query by the Committee, the Secretary, Deptt. of Telecommunications stated that soon after the amendment of law, two things would follow. Firsts that Department of Telecommunications would set up this authority by means of a Resolution of the Government. Secondly the Department would issue a notification that the authority set up under that Resolution is vested with the powers of the Director-General of Telecommunications under Section 4 of the Indian Telegraph Act in respect of certain matters. Once that is done, the authority would be clothed with the powers of Telegraph Authority in relation to its are a of work. However, it would still be a creature of the executive arm of the Government. Later after an year or so it will come before the Parliament with a comprehensive Bill.

In reply to a query regarding the impact of Telecom Regulatory Authority after its inception on working of Telecom Network in the country, the Ministry informed that it was excepted that the Telecom Regulatory Authority would have healthy impact on the working of telecom services in the country, since it will act as a watch dog for telecom sector, ensure level playing field as also monitor quality of services and protect and promote the consumer interest.

Asked whether after setting up the Authority, it would be possible for Government to set aside any decision of the proposed Authority, the Secretary Deptt. of telecoommunications replied in negative. He further added that the intention was that there would be not right of appeal to the executive wing of the Government. The orders issued by the proposed Telecom Regulatory Authority can only be challenged before the High Court or the Supreme Court.

In the light of the Government view known to the Committee, the Committee agree with the amendment of Section 3(6) of Indian Telegraph Act, 1885 for inclusion of any statutory or non-statutory authority within the definition of Telegraph Authority and support the Bill. The Committee hope that steps will be taken to set up a statutory Authority.

Science & Technology Development

The investment in Research and Development. (R & D) has increased from a paltry Rs. 20 crore in the First Five Year Plan. Presently there are 214 universities, 400 national laboratories and 1300 in-house R & D centres in the industrial sector. Several Science & Technology departments have been set up in the areas of environment, non-conventional energy resources, bio-technology, ocean development, industrial research, space, atomic energy, defence, health, agriculture and electronics.

Identification and promotion of priority areas in R & D is done by Science an Engineering Research Council (SERC) set up under the Department of Science & Technology (DST). DST supports 12 autonomous research insitutions as well, for furthering research work in several discipline. Technology Information, Forecasting and Assessment Council (TIFAC) has been set up for generating technology forecasting and technology assessment documents and enabling a technology information system that is interactive and nationally accessible.

Industrial research in several diverse fields of scientific activity is being undertaken through a network of 40 laboratories and 81 field stations set up by the Council for Scientific and Industrial Research (CSIR). In the field of bio-technology, more than 24 specialised R & D centres have been developed for pursuing state-of-the-art research. Identical efforts for promoting new avenues of research are being undertaken in the field of ocean development as well.

The Union Budget for 1996-97 has taken various measures to promote R & D facilities. A matching one time grant has been awarded to CSIR and the Indian Council of Agricultural Research (ICAR) for modernisation of laboratories and institutes. The Technology Development and Application Fund created in 1995-96 has been proposed to be strengthened by Rs. 30 crore. A Five Year Tax Holiday under Section 80-IA of the Income Tax Act has been allowed to companies exclusively create for participation in R & D activities. The existing procedure for awarding weighted deduction under Section 35(2AA) of the Income Tax Act on sums paid for scientific research to a National Laboratory or a University or an IIT has been amended, by deleting the condition of approval by an outside body. In order to encourage R & D efforts, goods developed and patented in India and concurrently in specified countries have been exempted from levy of excise duty for a period of 3 years. The exemption procedure for customs duty on import of equipment and consumables for R & D institutions has been rationalised as well.

Private Sector Partcipation

The Value added service sector has been open to the private sector since 1992. In respect of value added services, except radio paging and mobile telephony services, companies registered in India are permitted to operate under licence on non exclusive basis. In the area of Radio paging and Cellular Mobile Telephone Services, however, a policy of selection is being followed in the granting of licences through a system of tendering.

A tender for operation of radio paging services in 27 cities was earlier invited and 14 companies have been granted operating licences. For other areas of the country comprising 19 territorial telecom circles, tenders have been invited, and licensing is being progressively done. Commercial service has been started in 22 cities by one or more operators to over 48,000 subucribers and in the rest of the five cities the service will start very soon.

Eight companies have been selected for the franchises of cellular mobile service in the four metro cities namely Bombay, Delhi, Calcutta and Madras. In respect of rest of the country, a tender had been invited. The evaluation of 33 bids for the 20 telecommunications circles, is expected to be completed shortly. Service has commenced in Calcutta and Delhi in September 1995.

With a view to supplement the efforts of Department of Telecommunications in providing telecommunication services to the people, 81 bids received for grant of licence for operation of basic services in 20 telecom Circles are now under evaluation.

The government has decided to create an autonomous Telecom Regulatory body called the Telecom Regulatory Authority of India (TRAI). This will have well defined functions, responsibilities and powers to play the role of a watch-dog body for the telecommunications sector in an effective manner. The Authority will regulate its procedure for conduct of business with the approval of the government and will be expected to ensure transparency and accountability.

Profound changes are taking place in Telecommunication sector the world over and India is no exception. The Government of India has taken bold initiatives to liberalise and expand the telecom network in the country.

Some of the milestones in this direction are:

— 1984

Manufacture of Customer Premises Equipment delicensed.

— 1991

New Industrial Policy permitting private sector to manufacture all types of telecommunications equipment.

Other salient features are:

No industrial Licence is required;

Automatic approval of foreign equity investment up to 51 per cent in the case of manufacturing projects:

Automatic approval of foreign collaboration in the case of telecommunications sector with technology fees up to Rs. 10 million net of taxes and/or royalty up to five per cent for domestic sales and/or eight per cent for exports.

The possibility for more than 51 per cent foreign equity and higher technology fees/royalty in manufacturing projects through special approvals;

All foreign investment proposals for telecommunications services require the specific approval to the Government of India.

1992

Value added services thrown open to private sector participation.

1994

New National Telecommunications Policy allowing private sector participation in basic services announced.

The National Telecommunications Policy announced by the Government would be instrumental in bringing about phenòmenal expansion and improvement in the telecom sector.

The objectives of the Telecommunications Policy are:

— providing Telecommunications for all and Telecommunications within the reach of all;

— Universal Service Obligation at affordable and reasonable price;

— Providing telecommunications services of world standard;

— To ensure that India emerges as a major manufacturing base and major exporter of telecom equipment.

The targets laid down in the policy are as follows:

— Telephones to be available on demand by 1997;

— All vjillages to be provided with telecommunications services by 1997;

— In urban areas a Public Calling Office (PCO) should be provided for every 500 persons by 1997;

— Special emphasis on the quality of telecoommunications services provided to the customers will be given;

— All value added services available internationally to be introduced in India, preferably by 1996.

The other important aspects of the policy are:

— Private initiative would be used to supplement the departmental efforts to raise additional resources both through increased internal generation and adopting innovative means, like, leasing, deferred payments, build-operate-and-transfer, build-lease-and-transfer.

— A suitable funding mechanism for indigenous R&D is proposed to be set up;

— Pilot projects will be encouraged directly by the government in order to access new technologies, new systems in both basic as well as value added services.

With low telephone penetration rates, India represents one of the world's most attractive markets for telecommunications service providers and equipment manufacturers. Service sector opening of the basic telecom services to the private sector is the biggest opportunity for foreign direct investment. The growth potential in the basic telephone service in India is tremendous taking into consideration the low telephone density at present.

The challenge in rural telecommunications in India is indeed quite formidable. Out of the 604 734 villages in the country, only 185000 have telephone facility. Over 420,000 villages are still without a telephone facility.

Under the National Telecommunications Policy, one public telephone will be provided in each of the over half a million villages by 1997. Provisioning of a single telephone in each village, as per the telecom policy, may involve an investment of the order of S billion US Dollars. The sub-sector of value added services is already open for private investment. This sector in India represents one of the world's largest opportunities for supply of services and equipment.

The Indian Switching market, which is estimated to increase from about 2.5 million lines now to over 3.00 million lines in 1996-1997 represents-one of the largest market in the Asian region. The digital switching markets in India has witnessed a true metamorphosis since 1991 when the new Industrial Policy was announced by the Government.

A number of foreign companies attracted by DOT's liberalised procurement policies, have set up local production ventures in India. The opening up of the Import Policy in 1992 has opened this largest market to international competition.

The market for providing private networks is also growing very fast. Major international companies have already announced their plans for making an entry in this market.

The Radio Transmission Equipment market in India has undergone extensive changes in the post industrial liberallization period. With the diversification or production of transmission equipment which was earlier limited to the public sector companies, the present production base has expand with the setting up of the manufacturing facilities in the private sector.

With the opening up of Microwave Radio systems to competition, a number of multinational companies have entered the radio equipment market. The digital microwave radio equipment market has potential for large investments since most of the radio frequency spectrum in microwave is still available for deployment.

The investment opportunities in the optical fibre cable and equipment as well as infrastrucure equipment for value added services such as cellular and paging are immense. With the possibility of the entire long distance network being converted to optical fibre media, a number of international companies are getting their products validated at present. The investment opportunities in this area are extremely good.

Another area expected to sustain great demand in the coming decade is VSATs with voice transmission. The steady increase in the number of customers demanding high bit rate data transmission and separate corporate networks has given spur to VSAT development.

With increased availability, VSAT services are likely to get a big push and, therefore, the opportunities in this sector are excellent.

— The gross receipts of the Department of Post during the year 1995-96 were Rs. 1150 crore. Gross working expenses were Rs. 2472 crore and net working expenses Rs. 1810 crore. there was, therefore, a deficit of Rs. 660 crore. During the year 1996-97, as per budget estimates, the gross receipts are expected at Rs. 1350 crore and gross working expenses at Rs. 2616 crore. With net working expenses at Rs. 1962 crore the deficit is estimated at Rs. 612 crore for 1996-97. (BE).

— The Budget of Department of Post has been in deficit continuously over the years, and no dividend is being paid to the general revenue. Modernisation activities, through inductin of new technoloy, has been initiated on a modest scale during the current plan. Its further expansion and spread during the next plan, are likely to improve the service efficiency. A modernised postal system should also be able to provide new value added services to yield revenue. Low tariff on most of the postal services for many years, and inadiquate agency charges for agency functions, are the main factors for the deficit. However, a moderate increase in some of the services i.e., printed postcard from 60 paise to 100 paise and registration fee from Rs. 6.00 to Rs. 8.00 and introduction of cmpetition postcard at Rs. 2.00 each is expected to yield additional revenue to the tune of Rs. 76 crore in a full financial year. The degree of subsidy, as indicated in Table 2.11 ranges from about 1 per cent in respected of money orders to 92 per cent on postcard.

— The network owned and operated by the Department of Telecommunications (DOT) has been generating surpluses, which is utilised for further exapansion of the net work. Net receipts increased to Rs. 4951 crore in 1995-96 (RE) from Rs. 3936 crore in 1994-95 reflecting an increase of 25.8 per cent. Net receipts are estimated at Rs. 5213 crore in 1996-97 (BE). The dividend contribution to the general revenues increased to Rs. 279 crore in 1995-96 (RE) from Rs. 270 crore in 1994-95. The operating ratio, which is a percentage of net operating expenses (excluding the provision for redemption of bonds) to operating revenue earned (excluding registration fee) has come down to 48.7 in 1995-96 (RE) from 48.8 in 1994-95. The plan outlay for Telecommunication Services (including all PSUs) for the year 1996-97 (BE) is marginally higher at Rs. 9874 crore from Rs. 9830 crore in 1995-96 (RE). The entire outlay (except Rs. 5.00 crore pertaining to WMo etc. which is by way of budgetary support) is to be financed from the internal accruals and extra budgetary resources of the Telecommunication sector. Internal accruals amounting to Rs. 7491 crore account for 75.9 per cent of total resources against 79.6 per cent in 1995-96 (RE).

— Though the telecom network in India is fairly large in absolute terms, (in 1994 it was ranked fourteenth in the world) yet the tele density was 1.4 per cent in March, 1996. An advanced and efficient telecommunications system can enhance international competitiveness of the economy. The DOT has been increasing the quantum of resources deployed for the development of the telecom infrastructure, although the pattern of financing has undergoes a sea change. During the first plan DOT received budgetary support which accounted for around 79 per cent of the total resouces deployed it. In the Eighth Plan, 78.7 per cent is expected from internal accruals, 21 per cent from borrowings and other sources, and only 0.3 per cent from budgetary support. In the coming years, substantial investment would be required to upgrade and expand the existing telecom network. The aggregate resource requirements for the provision of basic and cellular mobile telecom services as estimated bny the Expert Group on Commercialisation of Infrastruture Projects is placed at Rs. 1,91,500 crore by 2006. Thee estimates are at todays prices and duty structure.

— Of late, DOT has primarily relied on internal accruals. However, to meet its targets of network expansion, DOT will have to look to a larger resource pool. It will have to devise a tariff structure which largely reflects the cost oriented approach, subject to country's social obligations and thrusts.

— A corporate structure for the DOT will enable it to leverage its substantial assets and raise adequate funds to meet all its investment needs. Corporate structure would makè DOT into an autonomous entity owned by the Government. In the short and medium term, the government will remain the dominant operator and provider of telecom services in the countrty. However, with the advent of private operators, the present tariff regime should orient as quickly as possible towards a costbased structure. It is imperative to have the tariffs reviewed to allocate costs for various services and identify the need, if any, of subsidies.

— As per the revised estimates for 1995-96, the total expenditure on Broadcasting was Rs. 974 crore as against total receipts of Rs. 549 crore. This shows an increase of 19 per cent and 20.4 per cent in total expenditure and receipts, respectively. As a result, the ratio of total receipts to total expenditure improved from 55.8 per cent in 1994-95 to 56.4 per cent in 1995-96. The rising trend in commercial receipts in broadcasting activity over the past few years is indicative of efforts being made in this direction. Commercial receipts were Rs. 426 crore in 1993-94, Rs. 450 crore in 1994-95, and Rs. 540 crore in 1995-96 (RE). Further break up of commercial receipts brings to the fore the overwhelming contribution of Doordarshan towards revenue generation. The commercial receipts in case of Doordarshan were Rs. 363 crore in 1993-94, Rs. 384 crore in 1994-95 and Rs. 460 crore in 1995-96.

— The important place commanded by India in world trade in coffee, tea, leather and spices on a historical basis has continued in recent years as wll. In 1994, India accounted for 2.4 per cent, 13.6 per cent, 2.5 per cent and 9.1 per cent of world trade in coffee and coffee substitues, tea and mate, leather, and spices, respectively. Furthermore, there has been a significant progress in export diversification, and India has emerged as an important exporter of iron ore and concentrates, and pearis, precious and semi-precious stones. In 1994, India accounted for 6 per cent or world exports of iron ore and concentrates and 10.9 per cent of world exports of pearls, precious and semi precious stones (Source: 1994 United Nations International Trade Statistics Year Book, 1995).

— During 1950, India accounted for about 1.8 per cent (1.85 per cent of exports and 1.71 per cent of imports) of world trade. After gradually declining to 0.57 per cent by 1980, India's share improved marginally to 0.63 per cent by 1985. The reason for improvement in the share was that while world trade declined in the period 1980-85, India's trade continued to grow. However it came down again to 0.53 per cent by 1991. The first half of the nineties witnessed a sharp increase in India's exports and imports have grown in dollar terms annually by 12.4 per cent and 9.4 per cent, respectively. The corresponding growth rates of world trade was about 5.7 per cent. The secular decline in India's share in world trade has been arrested and reversed, and the years ahead are likely to see a continuation of this increasing trend.

— The trade policy components of the reform process undertaken since July 1991 have been motivated by a full recognition of the important role that trade can play in promoting growth. The utilisation of the expanded scope for specialising in areas of comparative advantage is manifest in the improved growth performance of the economy. Furthermore, while exports have vigorously responded to the removal of the anti-export bias of a protectionist environment, domestic industry appears to have been stimulated by the expended availability of imported inputs and capital goods as well as the challenge of competing in the international market place. The positive response of Indian industry to liberalisation is amply demonstrated by the capital goods sector. The tariff on capital goods was as high as 85 per cent in the pre-reforms period. This has been reduced to about 25 per cent covering about 80 per cent of capital goods in 1995-96. The capital goods industry which witnessed a negative growth of 12.8 per cent in 1991-92, registered an average growth of about 23 per cent during 1994-96.

— The terms of trade, which measure the terms of exchange between a unit of exports and a unit of imports, have been improving in the post-reform period. Two common ways of measuring the terms of trade are the net terms of trade (NTT) and the income terms of trade (ITT). A time series indicating all parameters of terms of trade (TOT) for India since 1969-70 with the base of 1978-79 = 100 Indicates that there have been wide fluctuations in the TOT. The NIT (1978-79=100), which is an index of export prices divided by an index of import prices, improved from 109.3 in 1990-91 to 152.4 in 1994-95. It is

— It may be mentioned that India s purchasing power of exports as reflected thorough ITT has been improving continuously since 1985- 86. The value index of exports at 484 stands much higher than that of imports at 351 and hence, in terms of value, india has gained.But in terms of volume, the index of exports has been much less at 384 in comparison to that of imports at 515. This means that the volume of imports is increassing faster, though India is getting a better price for her exports.

— Compared to the experience of other developing countries, the improvement in the terms of trade for India has been very impressive. The NTT (1990=100), as presented in the UN's International trade Statistics Year Book, 1995, is reproduced below:

— Developing economies, with exports dominated by primary products, lost out to developed econoies,. Relavtive abundance of supply of primary products as well as the superior bargaining strength of developed countries have often ben adduced as two major reasons for the deterioration in the terms of trace. Gains in the terms of trade for India in the comparable period perhaps reflects her diversified export base as well as the relatively low international prices of oil in the relevant period.

India is committed to further liberalisation of its import regime, notwithstanding the dismantling of licensing controls over a wide area. At the same time, there are concerns whether developed nations of the world are implementing in letter and spirit their part of the obligations under the Uruguay Round Agreements. Many contries are resorting to protectinist devices in the guise of environmental hazards and exploitation of labour such as child labour. The obligations of providing access to imports of developing countries, especially textiles and garments, are being circumvented under one pretext or the other, even under the back-loaded integration of Textiles and Clothing into the World Trading System. Such restrictions are designed to keep out cheaper imports.

By virtue of the radical shift from a highly-regulated to an outward-oriented economy, India has attracted immense interest abroad, at both Governmental and private investor levels. India is one of the largest emerging markets, second only to China's, and the country has been experiencing inflows of foreign portfolio and direct investments—thought not as large as in China and a few other countries—which were unthinkable in the world of even 1980s. Economic strength has become the principal determinant of a nation's standing in the international community, and even the most powerful country, the United States of America, looks for market opportunities all over, more especially in the dynamic Asia-Pacific region, as the best shield of security.

With the end of the Cold War, the East-West barriers have broken down. The rapid spread of liberalisation and globalisation is a historic development which has blurred both East-West and North-South divisions. Developing countries have been compelled to adapt themselves to conditions of global interdependence although in the process they run grave risks in the medium-term and rare not assured of international safety nets.

In the rapidly changing world environment, each developing country must certainly concentrate on building its inherent strength and developing areas of comparative advantage and forge alliances with neighbours and, where promising, enter regional blocs which offer greater opportunities of trade and other exchanges to enhance national arena, disadvantaged nations must make common cause and unite to advance their pressing needs more effectively than what has been witnessed over the last fifty years in the post-decolonisation era. This is the only way of securing a post-cold war order which is just and equitable.

India has a long way to go before it could emerge as a strong global player, as currently it occupies the 32nd place as a leading exporter of merchandise, well below several countries in East and South-East Asia. It has to make up for the time lost in its inward-looking route to development which left the cuntry far behind in the international league, despite building a strong industrial base and possessing highly technical manpower, the third largest in the world. Indian planning did not take sufficient note of the gathering pace of global intergration with the frowth of merchandise trade exceeding the growth of output in virtually every year of the post-war period.

In recent years, India has begun to look East, is now a full dialogue partner in ASEAN (the 7-member Association of South East Nations) and excepts to find a place in the Asia Pacific Economic Forum (APEC) by 1999. These should promote greater intra-Asian trade and investment flows even as India strives to gain an increasing share of exports into developed economies of the West such as the European Union and North America. Trade with Russia and Eastern Europe as well as Central Asian States holds prospects of considerable expansion over present levels and a more promising development is the initiative taken by 14 states of the Indian Ocean Rim for an economic cooperation grouping with a Charter expected to be signed in March 1997.

The bilateral and pluralistic approaches cannot, and should not, in any way dilute India's firm commitment to multilaterialism which is the best safeguard against domination of the global economy by a few powerful nations. India's immediate responsibility is to solidify South Asian cooperation through SAPTA and ensure its early graduation to becomes SAFTA (South Asian Free Trade Area) to make it a region of good neighbourliness less prone to conflilcts than at present. With 16 per cent of the world's population, India's weight in the international economy remains negligible, and the building up of internal strength with determination through higher saving, and investments and greater efficiency in the use of resources is a pre-requisite for the country to claim its due share in the global market-place.

Looking Ahead

The fifth decade of Independence has triggered investment interest in India as never before. Policymakers should now bring in a lot more clarity on their objectives.

The rules of international trade have changed. Witrh trade barriers getting dismantled by the day, there is need to infuse a very high degree of competitiveness. A major development is the evolution of regional trade groupings like the European Community (EC), the North American Free Trade Association (NAFTA), ASEAN, APEC etc.

Though the south Asian countries have formed the SAARC, progress achieved in free trade among these has been slow. Apart from mere trade flows, potential benefits in terms of the phasing out of poliltical animosities and more cohesive regional developments are immense.... The EC experience proves this. Over the last 50 years Britain, France and Germany, who have been bitter adversaries for centuries, have been bonded together on the strength of mutuality of economic interests. The SAARC union could grow to include China, the Central Asian Republics and the Indian Ocean rim countries, including South Africa, and forge close links with ASEAN and APEC in course of time. The comparable levels of economic development of most of the countries in this region would help in co-ordinated growth.

There is a huge market for such equiptment: there are capabilities in these countries to produce entire range of such equipment–generators, turbines, boilers, transformers, switchgears, motors etc.

The Korean automobile manufacturers—Daewoo Motors and Hyundai—indicate plants for developing India as a major centre for their global operations. Like we did in regard to Maruti, in the assimilation of mass production technology, India should attempt absorption of the high productivity levels of the Koreans, Americans and others; combine this with the strength of the massive availability of skilled manpower to win global markets.

With the progress of economic reforms in many countries of the world and deregulation of financial markets, the importance of private capital flows into Asia has increased from US $ 76.8 billion in 1994 to US $ 98.0 billion in 1995, while net official flows increased marginally from US $ 5.6 billion to US $6.4 billlion during the same period. Similarly, while there were considerable official flows to Mexico and the transition countries in 1995 in support of their comprehensive adjustment programmes, net private capital flows to the developing countries increased from US $ 140.4 billion in 1994 to US $ 166.6 billion in 1995. India has has modest, but increasing, success in attracting a growing part of these private capital flows. Furthermore, much of these private capital inflows into India has been of the non-debt creating variety, and helped to boost the balance of payments as well as the availability of investible resources in the economy.

The international financial community is appreciative of India's economic performance in the last years, but concerns continue to be expressed about the high fiscal deficit, the slowing down of structural reforms, continued restrictions on consumer goods imports, and tariff levels considerably higher than in other countries. Also, references are often made to India's move towards capital account convertibility (with some observers advocating a cautions approach), high level of subsidies, inadequate disinvestment in the public sector, need for further relaxation of rules to attract foreign investment and the continued high stake of the government in the public sector banks. On the whole, the international community is very positive about India's effort to achieve a high rate of growth.

Participants in the India Development Forum (IDF) meeting in September 1996 acknowledged the strong performance of the Indian economy and appreciated the new Government's declaration to continue reform measures to strengthen the social programmes as set out in the Common Minimum Programme (CMP). Various delgates stressed the importance of (i) fiscal consolidation, (ii) sustaining programmes in the social sectors, (iii) infrastructrue, (iv) provety eradication, (v) reforms in agriculture, public sector, and financial sector, and (vi) strengthening of legislation against child labour. In support of India's economic development, the donor countries pledged official assistance in 1996-97 of US $ 6.7 billion. Inclusion of US $ 400 million in long-term finance, promised on a bilateral basis at market rates, will raise this total to above US $ 7 billion. About 33 per cent of the total could be in the form of grants and interest-free loans.

With effect from January 1, 1997, India subscribed to the Special Data Dissemination Standards (SDDS) of the International Monetary Fund (IMF). by subscribing to the SDDS, India ha committed itself to streamilining the tatistical system of the country to produce most of the data categories with a much shorter time lag, improved quality and coverage by December 31, 1988.

By virtue of the radical shift from a highly-regulated to an outward-oriented economy, India has generated immense interest abroad, but it has a long way to go before emerging as a strong global player, opines the author. India's development strategy launched in the 1950s, soon after Independence, aimed mainly at strengthening the industrial base of the country, especially in basic goods and heavy machine-building, and adopted the import-substituation model to achieve self-reliance. Exports were not viewed as an integral part of overall economic development, and such imports as became unavoidable were financed by drawing down foreign exchange reserves that had accrued to India at the time of Independence, in the form of sterling balances held in its favour for goods and services provided by this country during the Second World War.

Export pessimism dominated the mood of the early planners as it was rightly assumed then that until India's manufactures began to be diversified, there was little possibility of exporting manufactures while primary products and traditional manufactured goods faced poor demand prospects in the world market. It was during the later half of the fifties, when the Second Five Year Plan was under way with its emphasis on heavy industry, largely in the public sector, that it began to be realised that India needed to export to be able to finance at least part of the maintenance and developmental imports.

The foreign exchange crisis that was looming by mid-1957 reinforced the importance of export growth as part of planned development. The pessimistic view about the potential for export earnings gave way to a more positive approach in the Third Plan (1961-66) with the introduction of export promotion measures without deflecting from the thrust of import subsitution and industrialisation. It was clear by mid-estimated the import content of the inward-looking path of development opted by India. Pressures on balance of pyaments had already brought into existence the Aid-India-Consortium comprising the World Bank and developed countries interested in providing assistance to India. Renewed emphasis on exports was laid in the Fourth Plan (1969-74) which envisaged porogressive elimination of dependence on foreign aid while the Fifth Plan (1974-79) identified certain sectors such as engineering goods, garments, leather manufacture and marine products for achieving increases in exports.

Thus, as agianst virtual stagnation in the 1950s, export performance improved to an average growth of 3 to 4 per cent in the 1960s, and was more impressive in 1970s with an average growth of 6.3 per cent in volume and 15.9 per cent in value terms.

But in the three decades, India's share in world exports had declined throughout from about 2 per cent in 1950 to 0.65 per cent in 1970 and dropped further to 0.42 per cent in 1980. This was the period when there was impressive growth in world trade and the opportunities were seize by many smaller Asian developing countries as well as the industrialising economies in Latin America to great advantage.

Paradoxically, even as india's export growth was being maintained or marginaly improved upon, her share of world exports was declining. Over the three decades ending the Seventies, the share of exports in Gross Domestic Product (GDP) ranged from 4 to 6 per cent. In a continental economy of India's size, the role of external sector in the development process was under-played so much that it took a successions of droughts, oil price shocks and balance of payments difficulties in the first two and a half decades of planning before the country could begin to see import substitution and export promotion as two sides of the same coin. But heavy reliance on quantitative restrictions on trade through import and export controls and detailed industrial licensing kept India a closed economy.

The Primary issuance of securities has a long history in India. The Indian bond market, measured by the estimated value of bonds outstanding, is next only to the Japanese and the Korean bond market in Asia. By January 31, 1995, the outstanding value of the Indian securities market was estimated to have reached Rs.3000 billion, almost 3.5 times its size in 1986. The size is deceptive as, despite attractive yields, secondary market trading has remained poor with virtually no quotation even in respect of listed securities. The estimated outstanding amount accounts for about 42% of GDP, as at the end of January 1995. Partial deregulation of interest rates in the early nineties and increasing emphasis on monetary policy in stabilization are the first major steps towards the emergence of an active debt market, with government securities spearheading the process. With the issuance of government securities at market determined coupon rates and the use of innnovative products, it has become possible, for the first time, for other issuers to offer debt products priced off the yield on government securities.

The process of financial sector reforms initiated in 1991, is far from complete. The Growth of the Indian Capital Market since Independence has been phenomenal. The number of stock exchanges increased from 7 in 1947 to 23 in 1994. Likewise the number of listed companies on stock exchanges grew from 1125 in 1946 to 7811 at the end of 994. Similarly, the quantum of listed capital registered a growth of about 565 times from Rs.27C crore in 1946 to Rs.152,322 crore at the end of March, 1994.

The basic objective of financial sector reforms is to promote a diversified, efficient and competitive financial system by a policy shift from detailed regulation and controls to one based on market forces. Alongwith dismantling administrative regulation, the goal is establishment of a system of prudential regulation, supported by a mechanism for reporting, monitoring and supervision of the compliance.

Another major plank of reform is injection of new competition into a hitherto virtually government owned financial system. For the first time in many years, six new banking licences have been granted to the private sector all of which have been implemented. The new banks are permitted to have financial joint ventures with fgoreign baks, particularly for accessing modern systems and technology. There has been a mushrooming of Non-Banming Finance Companies (NBFCs), some of whom have already built up a large net-work. Several well known investment banks have established a presence in India. Since April 1993, nearly 300 Foreign Institutional Inestors (FIIs) have been registered with the regulatory authority and quite a few are active investors in the domestic capital market which has been opened up to foreign portfolio investment in a limited way. Several new mutual funds have been set up by the private sector including some by global fund managers. The most spectacular growth has been registered when we compare the share of market capitalization to gross domestic products (GDP) which was 12.9% in 1946, while in 1991-92 it was 57.2% and further increased to 68.8% during 1993-98.

Trade Policy

Side by side with the announcement of New Industrial Policy for Promoting Small Tiny and Village Enterprises, the Government have also announced major reforms in the Trade Policy. The main objective of the trade policy have been to progressively reduce the system of administrative controls and lilcences and to link import except in the case of essential items. The major reforms in the Trade Policy are given below:

Exports were in the past allowed replenishment to provide for essential inputs required for the manufacture of products exported. To allow flexibility to enable diversification of export products and also as an incentive for exports, the REP licenses so issued, were allowed to be freely sold. The entitlement for REP licenses also varied from item to item. In view of the flexibility of the REP Licenses Government realise that to treat it as licence is an misnomer, under the new policy the REP licences have been replaced by a new instrument named 'Eximscrips'. Eximscrips will be issued on the basis of FOB value of exports or Net FOreign Exchange (NFE) earnings from exports as indicated below. The main features of the new systems are:

The basic rate at which Eximscripts will be issued against exports will be 30% of FOB value. Exports to hard currency areas will be eligible for Eximscrips valid for hard currency imports while exports to rupee payment areas will be issued Eximscrips valid for imports from these areas only. However, as a measure of transition, exports to rupee payment areas may continue to avail of REP licences valid for hard currency imports at the rate prevailing prior to 4th July, 1991. This transition facility will be available only for exports effected upto 31st December 1991.

Products such as gems and jewellery, handcrafts, newspapers, journals and periodicals and cinematographic films, which enjoyed higher rated of REP will receive Eximscrips at the same rates as before.

The Basis rate of 30% is inadequate for exports of certain products such as value-added agricultural projects, electronics, bulk drugs and marine products, formulations and certain categories of advanced engineering goods. These products will be eligible for an additional Eximscrips entitlement of 10 percentage points, taking the total Eximscrips rate to 40% of FOB value.

For exports made on the basis of duty free imports obtained against Advance Licences, Eximscrips will be available at the general rate of 30% but this will be applied to the net foreign exchange earnings. On the same principle. Eximscrips at 30% of NFE will also be available for all EOU and EPZ units.

The 30% of NFE rate of Eximscrips is also applicable to service exports, including software exports which is a thrust area. The definition of services covered under this category is being ratinallized and extended to include other services such as services of architects, textile designers, artists, management consultants, lawyers etc. The benefit will be available to services exported by resident Indians for which remittances are made to India. The details are being notified separately.

Eximscrips issued to exporters will be tradeable and can be used to import any item in the limited permissible list (Appendix-3), the non-sensitive canalised list (Appendix-5A) and for all OGL, items for actual users (Appendix-6, List 8, Part I and List 10). Eximscrips earned by exporters on their own exports can also be used to import non-OGL capital goods other than those on the restricted list (Appendix-1A). All REP licences issued against exports prior to 4th July, 1991 will continue to be valid for the life of the licence and will have the same import entitlement as the new Eximscrips. Additional licences issued to export houses/trading houses, which were earlier valid for a more limited range of imports, will also be valid for the same range of imports as Eximscrips.

With the introduction of Eximscrips, the system of issuing supplementary licences of raw material, components and spares listed in Appendix-3 will be discontinued except for small scale industries and for manufacturers of specified life saving drugs and equipment. In future, all import requirements of these items (with the exceptions indicated above) will be made through Eximscrips, Similarly items in Appoendix-4 and Appendix-9, which were earlier importable against supplementary licences, will henceforth be importable only against Eximscrips. Import of items appearing in Appendix-2 Part B (list of Restricted Items) and Appendix-8 (List of Scientific and Measuring Instruments Restricted for Import) of the Import-Export Policy 1990-93 will continue to require licences. Such licences as well as licences required for small scale industries and manufactures of life saving drugs/equipment will be called Special Licences as these will be limited and include special cases.

As a measure of import compression and to strengthen the linkage between import capability and exports, two further changes have been made. The category of unlisted OGL has been abolished and these items have been shifted to Appendix-3. They are now importable only against Eximscrips (except for SSI and manufacturers of life saving drugs and equipment). In the case of units subject to the Phased Manufacturing Programme (PMP), many of which benefit from concessional duty on their imports of OGL items, all such items will henceforth be importable only against Eximscrips.

Eximscrips will be issued only after export proceeds have been realised. The procedure for issue of Eximscrips has been streamlined and Government will ensure that Eximscrips are issued within 48 hours of the receipt of the application accompanied by single document, namely, the bank certificate for the realisation of export proceeds.

Advance Licences

The system of advance licences is designed to provide exporters with duty free access to the inputs they need to produce competitively for world markets. This is an important instrument of trade policy especially in our situation where tariff levels are still high. The Government has taken the following steps to strengthen the system of Advance Licences as an instrument of export promotion:

(i) The procedures for considering Advance Licence applications have been simplified to ensure that advance licences will be issued within 15 days of application in all cases where input-output norms have been fixed. Where norms have not been fixed, the licence will be issued within 45 days.

(ii) The number of documents accompanying an Advance licence application has been reduced from 9 to 3 where norms are prescribed and to 4 where they are not prescribed.

(iii) Ar present norms have been prescribed for 540 items. This will be increased to over 1000 items by 31st October, 1991 and more items will be covered thereafter.

(iv) Substantial Manufacturing Activity as a necessary condition under the Advance Licence Scheme will no longer be applicable for exports to the general currency area. However, the value addition norms will remain in force. A large number of exporters will benefit under this scheme.

(v) A new Scheme of Transferable Advance Licence has been introduced for GCA exports in selected thrust areas, namely textiles, leather goods and engineering industries. Under this scheme exporters can undertake exports based on duty paid inputs obtained from the market and subsequently obtain advance licences for replenishment of these inputs by duty free imports. These advance licences will be freely transferable. The coverage of the scheme will be extended on merits.

(vi) Advance licence will specify values in free foreign exchange both for the purpose of import and export. The currencies in which such values are denominated will be limited to those notified for this purpose by the RBI.

(vii) The Existing procedure for obtaining Bank Guarantee (BG) and Legal Undertaking (LUT) from different categories of exporters in being streamlined and liberalised as follows:

(a) Export/Trading/Star Trading House and Public Sector Undertakings will have the facility of obtaining advance licence against LUT only without any monetary limit.

(b) All manufacturing units having an annual turnover of at least Rs. 5 crores (including both domestic and exports turnover) during the previous 3 year would also be able to avail of the LUT facility up to a value limit of 50% of their annual production.

(c) A new unit without any production or export performance to its credit would also be allowed LUT facility provided it is promoted by an existing company with an annual production of Rs. 5 crores for more than three years. In such a case, both the new company and the promoting company would have to provide LUT.

(d) Bank guarantee and/or LUT obligation will be concurrent to the fulfilment of export obligation.

(viii) Exporters would be allowed to dispose of the materials imported against advance licences by way of replenishment without seeking prior permission of the licensing authority in cases where no MODVAT facility has been availed of on the domestic material used in exports.

(ix) Adjustment needed on account of fluctuation of prices of imported individual items would be permitted within the overall CIF value of advance licence.

(x) The power of revalidation which presently vests in the Licencing Committee at the Headquarters has been delegated to the Licensing Authorities.

(xi) In case where applications for an advance licence are turned down, the exporter will be permitted to convert to the Duty Drawback regime by the Collectors of Customs so that shipments made in advance can be imported on payment of duty subsequent claims of duty drawback.

(xii) Exporters can obtain advance release orders for domestic supply against advance licences under which the domestic supplier gets the benefit of deemed exports. Henceforth, release orders will be issued across the counter without requiring the name of the domestic supplier, which could be given later.

The adoption of these procedures would reduce discretionary controls and delays and afford much greater freedom to exporters in procuring essential duty free raw materials to maintain their competitiveness in the would market thereby promoting exports from the country.

The export Processing Zone scheme and the 100% EOU scheme were introduced to provide for duty-free enclaves, which would enable entrepreneurs to concentrate on production exclusively for export. However, with increasing liberalisation in the DTA, the duty advantages enjoyed by EPZs/EOUs have become less important. While the procedures of Customs Bonding are very onerous. The schemes have not therefore taken off as expected and they have also not attracted foreign investment aimed at tapping export markets to the extent that was expected. The working of these schemes has been reviewed and the following changes made:

(i) All EOUs/EPZ unit will be eligible for Eximscrips at the basic rate of 30% applied to net foreign exchange earning.

(ii) The duty applicable on DTA sales from EOUs/EPZ units is being reduced to 50% of the normal customs subject to the duty payable not being less than the excise duty on the same product. The extent of DTA sales allowed will be accordance with their entitlement. DTA sales will be permitted in the ratio of 25:75 in relation to export sales in case of units while use of indigenous raw material is more than 30% of production. In all other cases the ratio of permissible DTA sales to export sales will be 15:85. The procedures for clearing goods from the EOU/EPZ units for DTA sales are also being streamlined.

(iii) In order to encourage exporters to set up EOUs or EPX units the net foreign exchange earned by EOUs or EPZ units can be clubbed with the earnings of their parent/associated companies in the DTA for the purpose of according Export House. Trading House of Star Trading House status for the latter.

(iv) The IPRS scheme for supply of steel to exporters will also be extended to EOUs and EPZ units. The

Development Commissioners are being empowered to issue "payment authorities" in lieu of JCCI & Es.

Under the New Industrial Policy, most industries do not require an industrial licence except for a defined list. With a view to bringing about comparable streamlining in the procedure for EOU/EPZ approvals, a systems of automatic approvals is being established for all proposals which fall within certain parameters. Capital goods imports will be allowed under the automatic approvals procedure if they are fully covered by foreign equity or if they do not exceed 50% of the value of plant and equipment subject to a ceiling of Rs 3 crores. All proposals within the automatic approval parameters will be cleared within two weeks. All other proposals will be submitted to the Board of Approvals for consideration and decisions including issue of licences will be taken within 45 days.

A large number of issues relating to the operation of EOUs/EPZ units required centralized clearance in the Ministries of Commerce and Industry. Powers are being delegated to the Development Commissioners so that these approvals can be given on a decentralised basis. The specific approval of the Development Commissioner would not be required in cases of broad banding by EPZ units, where value addition is being maintained. The unit concerned would need only to provide relevant information to the Development Commissioner.

The following specific concessions to EOUs/EPZ units have also been extended:

(i) Allowing entry of imported raw material on "Provisional Assessment" basis, to expedite customs clearance.

(ii) Permitting units under the EPZ and EOU schemes to supply/transfer finished goods among themselves.

(iii) Replacement of multiple bond by a single bond, for obtaining import clearance.

(iv) Increasing the list of items under the "Special Imprest Licence Scheme" on selective basis.

(vi) Clarifying that containers stuffed in EPZ and EOUs are not to be reinspected at other points, as long as seals are intact.

Government have also decided to allow private parties to establish bonded warehouses within EPZs for stocking and sale of duty free raw materials, components, consumables and spares to EPZ units and EOUs. This will cut down delay in obtaining supplies of duty free materials which are in constant and regular demand by exporters. The details of this scheme will be notified shortly.

Other steps announced in the new Trade Policy have been the simplification of procedures for import of capital goods, decanalisation of number of items which were previously canalised, permission to allow established exporters to open foreign currency accounts in approved banks, raise external credits, pay for export related imports from such accounts and credit export proceeds to such accounts, its decision to re-designate the office of the Chief Controller of Import and Exports as Directorate General of International Trade with the principal function being to promote of exports, and facilitation of imports to promote export trade.

The policy changes now being implemented imply substantial reduction in the extent of licensing and in the number of types of licences. Supplementary licences for import of items in Appendixes-3 (except for SSI and manufacturers of life saving drugs and equipment), 4 and 9 of the Import-Export Policy 1990-93 have been abolished. Additional licences which were issued as an incentive to Export Houses and Trading Houses will stand abolished with effect from 1st April, 1992 and the incentive will take the form of an additional Eximscrip entitlement.

To achieve optimal import containment in the context of the present Balance of Payments situation, several steps have been taken. One of these is the shift of many items which are on OGL to the limited permissible list.

With these changes, the policy for import of raw materials components and other inputs needed for production has been simplified. Most raw materials and other inputs (except for those on the Restricted List) can be freely imported either against Eximscrips or on OGL. Some raw materials continue to be canalised but in more of these cases requirements beyond those provided by the canalising agencies can be met through Eximscrips.It is the policy of the Government to move to a situation where imports of essential raw materials and components needed for industrial production are regulated through appropriate tariffs. However, in view of the Balance of Payments position which necessitates continued import containment, this cannot be done immediately. Many items must therefore remain on the limited permissible list, with imports permitted only against Eximscrips.

The medium term objective of the Government is to progressively eliminate licensing and quantitative restrictions on capital goods and raw materials/ components so that all these items can be placed on OGL save for a small carefully defined negative list. This shift is proposed to be achieved over a 3 to 5 year period. The Government will appoint a High Level Committee to work out the modalities of achieving this transition keeping in mind the Balance of Payments position and the need to rationalise the reduce tariffs progressively to provide Indian Industry with an appropriate environment to develop international competitiveness.

Industrial Policy and Trade Policy of the Government of India

Over the years the Government of India has been adopting various measures for the liberalisation of the Industrial Policy, for streamling the licensing and foreign collaboration procedures, for reducing the number of agencies which the prospective investors have to approach to get the necessary approvals, etc., with the objective of attracting more investment and technology transfer. On the 24th July, 1991 the Government tabled before Parliament the Statement on Industrial Policy, 1991, which was followed by the issuance of a Notification by the Department of the Industrial Development to implement the Policy Statement and a series of Press Notes to set out the changes in the existing system and procedure for obtaining industrial licenses and approval of proposals for foreign and for foreign testing of indigenous raw materials and products and indigenously developed technlogies.

The new Industrial Licensing Policy of the Government of India has exempted form the requirement of obtaining industrial licence all industries, except those reserved for the Public Sector (Schedule I to the the Notification), those in respect of which Idustrial Licensing is compulsory (Schedule II to the Notification) and those relating to the items reserved for exclusive manufacture in the small scale sector (Schedule III to the Notification).

The exemption from Industrial licensing is also subject to:

The proposed project (except in the case of a project relating to electronics, computer software, printing industry, industry located within an area designated as 'industrial area' by a State Government before the 25th July, 1991 or the small scale or the ancillary sector) being not located with 25 kilo meters form the periphery of the standard urban area limits of a city having a population of more than one million according to the 1991 census; and of the Central and the State environmental laws and regulations including local zoning and land use laws and regulations.

Units qualifying for exemption from industrial licensing in accordance with the foregoing conditions are required only to file a Memorandum in the prescribed form, before establishement of the project, with the Department of Industrial Development (Secretariat for Industrial Approvals) together with a crossed demand draft for rupees one thousand in favour of the Pay and Account Officer, Department of Industrial Development and another Memorandum in the prescribed form at the time of commencement of commercial production.

Small scale and ancillary units are required, as before, to be registered with the Director of Industries of the concerned State. Manufacturing units with an investment in plant and machinery up to Rs. 60 lakhs, ancillary units with an investment in plant and machinery up to Rs. 75 lakhs and units which are willing to undertake an export obligation to the extend of 30 per cent of their annual production by the third year with an investment up to Rs. 75 lakhs are eligible for small scale registration.

The new industrial policy of the Government of India has announced major liberalisation for attracting foreign investment in respect of a list of high priority industries (Annexure III to the Statement of Industrial Policy, 1991). Foreign equity investment up to 51 per cent will be allowed subject only to the condition that;

— The requirement of imported capital goods should be covered by the foreign equity;

— The amount of dividend payment may be converted by export earnings of such items recorded in Years prior to the payment of dividend or in the year of payment of dividend. This will be monitored by the Reserve Bank of India. However, such balancing will not be required beyond a period of seven years from commencement of production.

In all such cases the Reserve Bank of India has been authorised to issue automatic approvals of foreign investment and also grant exemption from the operation of the relevant sections of the Foreign Exchange Regulations Act, 1973.

14

Major Achievements

Integrated service digital network (ISDN) and 800K BHCA:- C-DOT has developed Integrated Services Digital Network (ISDN) capability for its exchanges. The ISDN interfaces, bearer services and supplementary services have been developed according to ITU-T and national standards. The TEC testing of ISDN, 800K BHCA handling capability and environmental testing of ISDN hardware with high performance processor (for 800K BHCA capability) card successfully completed at ITI Bangalore. A MAX-XL exchange with the ISDN and 800K BCHA capabilities has been installed in the field trial site at Yelahanka, Bangalore. TEC testing completed at the field trial site and the exchange is ready for commissioning. The ISDN software release (Rel.X2-1 -1 -1) had also been installed at some of the working sites in different configurations e.g. SMB-L, SBM-XL, MAX-L, MAX-XL.

Intelligent network(IN) services:- Intelligent Services provide immense value-addition and revenue earning potential for service providers and services to the subscribers get improved flexibly and economically. Some of the IN services are Freephone, Virtual Card Calling (VCC), Virtual Private Network (VPN), Premium Rate Services, Televoting and Universal Access Number. C-DOT has developed very cost effective total solution viz. Service Switching Point (SSP) and Service Control Point (SCP) functionality for provisioning of IN services.

The TEC evaluation for IN services (SSP and SCP) have been successfully completed. The IN services have also been commissioned in MTNL-Delhi and Mumbai and Indore(M.P.). The SCP has been installed at Bhikaji Cama Place in Delhi while SSPs are located at Bhikaji Cama Place (Delhi), Prabhadevi (Mumbai) and Inclore.

The IN solution based on C-DOT technology shall be deployed nation-wide during this financial year at Jaipur, Ahmedabad, Pune, Bangalore, Chennai, Hyderabad, Lucknow, Patna. C-DOT has already installed a SSP at Calcutta. All the SSPs in DOT network will be connected to the SCP at Calcutta via CCS#7 signalling network.

CCS#7 signalling system: CCS #7 (SS7) signalling has been awarded technology approval after successful completion of its field trials in C-DOT SBM, MAX-L, and MAX-XL exchanges. CCS#7 signalling can be implemented in the existing MAX-UMAX-XL exchanges by suitable hardware and software enhancements.

Technology Deployment in the Field

Max-XL:- Fifteen MAX-XL exchanges have already been commissioned in the network and some are under installation. Department of Telecom (DOT) has placed an order for 207.5K lines of MAX-XL exchanges on ITI, Bangalore. Besides, educational orders on C-DOT MAX-XL manufacturers (other than M/S ITI, Bangalore) for 5K lines each have also been placed.

Tax-XL:- TEC awarded technology approval for TAX-XL after successful field trials. Dispatch of equipment for 45K TAX-XL lines (in addition to 207.5K lines of MAX-XL orders placed on M/s ITI as indicated above) is also in the pipeline.

Number of C-DOT Switching Systems commissioned in the network

Switching systems

	Operational	
	Exchanges	*Lines (Lakhs)*
128 RAX	13500	12.00
256 RAX	8555	15.85
SBIVI RAX	2452	22.20
SBIVI TAX	200	1.40
MAX-L	338	13.77
MAX-XL	11	1.30
MAX-XL TAX	1	0.01
Expansion		
128 RAX	-	1.25
SBM RAX/MAX	-	2.82
TOTAL	25057	70.60

TDMA PMP system:- All the pending point related to software have been incorporated and upgraded software has been offered to TEC for revalidation. Department of Telecom (DOT) has placed an order on M/s ITI for supply of 2.5 systems.

VSAT systems:- Department of Science and Technology (DST) so far has placed an order for supply of 87 VSAT 16 Kbps systems and out of this order, 67 systems have been dispatched till date.

Field and manufacturing support:- C-DOT continued to provide product support to 25,057 switches with 7.0 million lines of C-DOT technology in the network in terms of upgradation, retrofitting and training to field staff. C-DOT continued its interaction with the manufacturers and field installations for providing all types of maintenance support. C-DOT in co-ordination with TEC conducted a seminar on TDMA-PM P to familiarise DOT officers with TDMA-PM P product so that first twenty-five systems being procured from M/S ITI can be installed and commissioned in a smooth manner. The seminar was followed by a visit to field trial site - Mysore where C-DOTTDMA-PMP equipment has successfully completed the field trial.

Projection for the period Jan'99 - March'99 (On-going Projects under Completion Stage)

V5.1/5.2 interface for C-DOT switches:- C-DOT worked on V5.2 interface, which is an emerging concept for connecting Access Network Product (ANP)to the main exchange. This interface can serve different type of interfaces including radio system of the "Wireless In Local Loop (WILL)".

C-DOT has implemented the standardized protocols related to V 5.1 / V 5.2 to interface access network with C-DOT switches. This will help in interconnecting various access technologies to C-DOT exchanges. TEC has successfully completed its validation. The field trial for V5 interface shall commence shortly.

Composite MUX (remote line concentrator):- A 120 line unit which will serve both analog and ISDN subscribers is under lab. Testing /development. The Composite MUX (C-MUX) is an Access Network (AN) product. As a Remote Line Concentrator (RLC)for as AN], it is connected to LE-Local Exchange (e.g. C-DOT DSS) using V 5.2 interface. The V5.2 interface consists of a single 2.048 Mbps link supporting 120 subscribers.

Synchronous digital hierarchy (SDH) systems:- These projects constitute a series of products namely, STM-1, STM-4, Digital Access Cross-connect .(DACCS) and Network Management System. The development of these products are in different stages of product cycle. The STM-1 is in the internal validation stage and it is scheduled for offer to TEC/QA evaluation during end of this financial year, whereas STM-4 and DACCS are in the lab. realization stage.

Digital enhanced cordless technology (DECT) system:- This system provides Wireless In the Local Loop (WILL) solutions both in the urban and in the rural scenarios. While one solution uses Base Station Controller (BSC), Base Station Units (BSU) and remote radio units, the other uses an interface card in the remote line of the TDMA system. The later can serve wireless subscribers instead of wired subscribers usually supported by TDMA. Both these systems are in the validation stage and scheduled for offer to TEC/QA evaluation during end of this financial year.

VSAT system:- In the field of satellite communication, C-DOT had already developed technology for C and Extended-C band. The products-MCPC and ISD 64 based on these technologies have been already evaluated and field tried by TEC. The technology for Ku-band is under validation/& advance phase of development and the products - MCPC and ISD 64 kbps VSATs in. Ku-band are expected to be available for TEC/QA evaluation during end of this financial year.

Standards and specifications

Generic requirements

GRs finalised

Optical Time Domain Reflectometer (Full feature& Mini); Optical power meter (Type A& B); Stabilised Light Source at 1310 nm and 1550 nm; 1.5 GHz Yagi Antenna; 7 GHz Sub-STM-11 microwave equipment; Voice Mail Service; PABX with wireless extensions; DID-PABX with wireless extensions; "U" Interface for ISDN; Requirements for Computerised Material Procurement Information system of CGMTS, Calcutta; V.34 voice band data modem; Interface for High speed Line Driver; Interface for Remote access Server; Hardware requirements for DoTSOFT, Store and Forward Fax service; Indian Script Code for Language Paging for

Hindi/Marathi; Indian Script Code for Language Paging for Gujrati; Digital Wireless Local Loop system for Rural Areas; TDMA PMP system of C-DOT; Electronic Locator System; 5 Pair/0.50 mm PIJF Under Ground Telecom Cables.

GRs revised/amended

Digital Mux Channel Systems for 2/8, 8/34, 2/34 and 34/140 Mbps; Digital Distribution Frame; 30 Channel PCM Mux; Uninterrupted Power Supply 1-7.5 KVA; Optical Attenuator; Optical telephone; Optical Splicing Machine; Single Mode Optical Fibre Jumper (Patch cord and Pig Tails); Optical Spectrum Analyzer; Single Mode Optical Fibre (raw material); 40m Narrow Base Tower; 15m Self Supporting Mast; Multi Channel Per Carrier Very Small Aperture Satellite Terminal; SDH microwave equipment in 4,6,11 GHz band; 2 GHz Grid paraboloid Antenna; 2 GHz Feeder Cable; 6 GHz, 7 GHz, 11 GHz and 13 GHz High performance Antenna; 6 GHz, 7 GHz, 11 GHz and 13 GHz Wave guide; Interface requirement of Primary rate Digital Signal at 2.048 Mbps between DOT and Licensed Service Providers; :Large size Local-cum-Tandern Digital Exchanges; Interface requirement of ISDN CPE; Service description for Analog Subscriber; Requirements for Computerised Material Procurement Information system of MM cell of DOT, National Internet Backbone; Interactive Voice Response System; Line Jack Unit; Electronic Telephone Instrument (TPS); Subscriber Service Unit for Calling Line Identification

Presentation; Formatted Terminal and Line Concentrator regarding bilingual/multilingual working; Boss-Secretary system; DIP Box for Internal and External use; Thermoweld Sleeves; Aluminium Canister for Thermoweld Joint; Cable Duct Sealing system; Aluminium Canister for TSF Joint; Adhesive PVC Tape, Cleaning Tissue, Adhesive Ployster; Tape, Silica Gel, and

Microcrystalline wax; GD Tubes for Internal and External use; MDF and protection arrangement for Rural Automatic Exchanges.

GRs withdrawn

Optical Time Domain Reflectometer (Old Issue, Jan. '94); Power Meter (Precision); Power Meter (Handy); Light Source; Multi Channel Per Carrier Very Small Aperture Terminal (issue Feb. '95); 7 GHz 34 Mbps Digital M/W equipment (Old Issue, Mar'92); 11 GHz 140 Mbps Digital M/W equipment (Old Issue, Jan'93); 140 Mbps M/W equipment in 6 GHz (extended C band) (Old issue, Jan'94); STD Coin Collection Box (Old issue); Quarter Modular Line Cord; Electronic Telephone Instrument (Decadia/ DTMF)); Add-on unit to Coin Box Telephone (CBT-80); Card Vending Machine (Old issue); Disposable Smart Card (Old issue); Monitoring and Control system for Direct Exchange Line; PIJF Quad Trunk/ Carrier Cables.

Engineering guidelines issued for

SMPS Power Plant; Infrastructure Assessment of Traders for VRLA battery; Storage/Transportation of VRLA batteries; 10 Channel Digital UHF equipment; IS GHz 8 Mbps microwave equipment; Technical instructions for testing GMPCS services at Pune; Technical details and acceptance testing procedure for parenting of CSED rack of El O-B switches to OCB switches; Synchronisation of exchanges in the Indian Telecom network; Use of C-DOT Network Synchronisation equipment 2.0 in C-DOT and E10-B exchanges; Use of STP in local CCS7 Network; PSTN Access from Inet. -

Testing field trial and evaluation of products

Managed Leased Data Network of M/S HTL; STM-1 PDH/SDH Analyser of M/s W & G Pvt. Ltd.; Bench and Chamber testing of ADM-1 of M/s ITI Naini, Allahabad; Bench testing of ADM-1 6 of M/S ITI Naini, Allahabad;

Assisted M/s UPTRON Powertronics Sahibabad in testing of 100A SMPS Power Plant; Testing of software for traffic analysis of EWSDTAX/Local exchanges; Wind Tunnel test for 15m mast; Evaluation of a 40m Narrow Base Tower (first product); Evaluation of Circular Polariser retrofit Wits for use with 2.4m VSAT antenna; Post field trial Test of MCPC VSAT, Testing of INSAT MSS System at Jayanagar Earth Station, Bangalore; Evaluation of DCME-500 system; Evaluation of 18 GHz 8 Mbps microwave equipment of Mls HFCL; XIPC tests of 11 GHz, 140 Mbps microwave equipment of Mls Natelco; S/W version 2-1-1 -1 of C-DOT in Lab; V5.1 Protocol system for C-DOT; V5.2 Protocol in S/W 1-5-1-2 for C-DOT system; 800K BHCA for C-DOT MAX-XL with software version 2-1 -1 -11; 1200K BHCA overload in MAX-XL for C-DOT, C-DOT ISP-SO2 Card in 256 Port RAX; Protocol test of Intelligent Network Application Part (INAP) for C-DOT SSP; Protocol test of SCCP for C-DOT SSP; Protocol test of Transaction Capability Application Part for C-DOT SSP; lab. testing of C-DOT SCP; Interworking tests of NEAX 61 E with OCB-283 TAX on CCS7 for national and International calls; Testing of ISDN features in NEAX61 E exchange; Lab testing of Analog- and ISDN supplementary Services in C-DOT switch; Testing of Patch in AXE- 10 system regarding implementation of 10 digits uniform CLI; Validation of ISDN V5.1 in new technology exchange; Testing of pending problems of EWSD system Gurgaon; Validation testing of ISDN features in C-DOT MAX-XL exchange at Yelhanka, Bangalore; Signalling connection and control Part (SCCP) test for SSP Functionality of AXE-10 Switch at Malleswaram Exchange, Bangalore; Technology approval of C-DOT Network Synchronisation Equipment for use in C-DOT MAX-L and C-DOT SBM exchanges and E10B exchanges; Interactive voice response system at Alwar; DOT SOFT package for customer's application; Management of Lease, Line Data Network; Testing of

X.25 PVC between ACX and PSX; Testing of Frame Relay Over lrioi, Low Bit rate Data Analyser; Data Terminal Test set; Testing for Internet Telephony; TDMA PMP system of C-DOT, DECT system of M/s Siemens at Noida; Electronic Locator System; Preliminary evaluation of permanently Lubricated HDPE pipes.

Synchronisation

Fundamental and Planning guidelines of Synchronisation for Transmission Network; Refurbishment of Cesium Clocks at Backup National Reference Clock Centre;

Field support/software development

SMPS Power Plant of M/s ITI installed at Telephone Exch. Saharanpur; SMPS Power plant at CIDCO and Up nagar Telephone Exch. Nasik of M/s RBDC; Software solutions for Y2K issues in El O-B system; Software patches for ND-NE correspondence, CLIP-A in El O-B system; Software developed for revenue leakage issues in El O-B exchanges; Software package developed for subscriber management in E10B and OCB-283 exchanges; Suppression of LAC in the meter reading TAXIL tape consequent on the implementation of 10 digit CLI; Implementation of 10 digits uniform CLI in El 0-13, AXE-1 0, OCB-283; A report prepared of misuse of Call forwarding facility by mobile operator; Copies of Commandir and Ell O-B maintenance advisor supplied to field units; Training given to the staff of DTTC, Hyderabad in installation of New Type of Drop Wire Accessories and termination of 0.5 mm SS Drop Wire.

Field problems solved

SDH microwave Link on Lucknow-Sitapur route; Conversion of 34 Mbps Radio system from Analog Wideband 6 GHz to Digital in Jamnagar-Rajkot section; The interlinking of Indo-Bangladesh; Point of Inter connect functionality in respect of detail billing on calling line identification and level 1 services; Implementation of

IMA software in Ell O-B exchanges; No Dial Tone during night peak hours in Arnbala Cantt. Ell O-B exch.; Interworking of OCB-283 and FETEX-1 50; Technical assistance provided to solve the problem of the following exchanges; OCHLA report in Bhopal and Allahabad; TAXIL in Arnbala; Wakeup service in Jhansi; Saturation of ROU file in Varanasi; Detailed Billing in Cuttak and Pune; Local Cum TAX functionality in Janpath E10-B TAX; Failures of calls to malicious number in E10-B exch. Bikaner, Amritsar and Jullandhar; Implementation of 10 digit CLI in Guwahati E10B exch.; Restoration of Akola E10-B Exch.; Introduction of Internet Service from Hisar to Ambala; FRCT file saturation in Kanpur El 0-13 TAX; Dynamic STD locking facility at Surat.

Networking planning engineering

Inter-TAX circuit requirements for the year 1998-99 as part of National TAX Traffic study; Calculation of traffic data for dependent stations of TAXs for the purposes of National TAX Traffic study; Calculation of traffic data for dependent stations of TAXs for the purposes of National TAX Study; Participation of Interference coordination meeting between:-(a) INSAT Satellite System with Russian Satellite System and INTELSAT, USA, (b) INSAT and Indonesian Network in WPC, (c) INSAT and JAPAN Network in Japan, (d)Australia and India in WPC, (e) India Administration and representative of EMARSAT Satellite Networks in WPC; Appraisal of the validation report of testing of 8 Mbps, 18 GHz equipment of M/s HFCL; Advice to Telecom. Commission regarding special conditions for tender for procurement of 13 GHz microwave equipment; Report submitted to TCHQ for Call completion Rate and technical instruction for level 1 TAX overflow Traffic Management in the Network; Prepared status of Synchronisation of Indian Telecom. Network; Prepared proposal on Internet Numbering.

Type approval issued

Type Approval	:	384
Interface Approval	:	234
Service Test Certificate	:	227
Source Compatibility	:	49

Anticipated achievements

Generic requirements

GRs to be finalised

Pasive Optical Network; Global Positioning Satellite Primary Reference Source Receiver; 100m Tower; Distance Learning Equipment via Satellite; Interface requirements of Closed Group KU band VSAT Networks; SDH Analyser; Accessories and Components for Antenna, Waveguides and feeder cables; 13 GHz SDH equipment; Extra Large Local Cum Tandem Cum Transit Switch; Gateway Switch; National Synchronisation Plan; Primary reference Clock Cesium Frequency Standards; Interface requirements of Router with TCPAP; ISCLAP for Regional Language; Telecom. Aids for disabled persons; PVC Insulated Copper Clad Steel Drop Wire.

Test schedule/test procedure

GPS Receiver; High Bit Rate Digital Subscriber Line; Conventional Power Plants; 13 GHz SDH equipment of HFCL; 10 Channel digital UHF equipment; 8 Mbps 18 GHz PDH equipment; Antenna, Waveguides and feeder cables; Radio instruments; Accessories and components of Antennas, waveguides and feeder cables; SDH Analyser; Digital Cable Fault Locator for Low Insulation Faults; Resistance and Insulation Resistance Tester; Electronic Locator System; TWF Sleeves and TW Canister; Sheath Connector Assembly; Splice Filling Compound; Cable Cleaning Liquid; Emery Strip; Water Blocking Powder; Adhesive Aluminium Foil; Sealant Tape.

Test schedule/test procedure

GPS Receiver; High Bit Rate Digital Subscriber Line; Conventional Power Plants; 13 GHz SDH equipment of HFCL; 10 Channel digital UHF equipment; 8 Mbps 18 GHz PDH equipment; Antenna; Waveguides and feeder cables; Radio instruments; Accessories and components of Antennas, waveguides and feeder cables; SDH Analyser; Digital Cable Fault Locator for Low Insulation Faults; Resistance and Insulation Resistance Tester; Electronic Locator System; TWF Sleeves and TW Canister; Sheath Connector Assembly; Splice Filling Compound Cable Cleaning Liquid; Emery Strip; Water Blocking Powder; Adhesive Aluminium Foil; Sealant Tape.

Testing/field trial and evaluation

ADM 4 M/s ITI, Naini; ADM-1 /4/16 PDH/SDH Analyser of M/s W & G Pvt. Ltd.; Passive Optical Network system at Ludhiana; Evaluation of 40m Narrow Base Tower; 6 GHz SDH equipment of HFCL; 11 GHz SDH equipment; 7 GHz 34 Mbps of PCL; Multipath fade simulator; DCME System of M/s HTL; Validation of switching equipment for 1.3m, 1.69m lines; C-DOT Internet; Equipment for APT - Multimedia Project; Irnplementation of Synchronisation as per national Plan; CDMA system of M/s Qualcom; First product testing of Boss Secretary System; Technology approval of subscriber Service Unit for Calling Line Identification Presentation of C-DOT; Permanently Lubricated HDPE pipes.

Field support

Compliance of Y2K issues of E10-13, C-DOT and New Technology switches; Over Load control for CSE of E10-13; Storage and retrieval of OMC log of E10-13.

Network planning engineering

Inter-satellite Interference Coordination.

Tender evaluation

High Voltage Lab; Mechanical Testing Lab; Cable testing Lab.

Other activities

Forecast of TAX circuit requirements (Capacity) for the year 2002 as a part of National Tax Stud, Release of software for traffic analysis of EWSD switches for field units; External Plant simulate Network; Spectrum management: Future requirements of frequencies by Telecom Operators.

Studies made

Propagation studies; EMC Studies; Radio Modem; Infra red links; LMDS; HDFS; High Altitude Platform Station; Cross Polar Interference Calculation; Number Portability; Fraud management in Telecom; Internet Traffic bypass; Call Centre; Call Completion rate.

Tyre approval to be issued

Type Approval	:	128
Interface Approval	:	78
Service Test Certificate	:	76
Source Compatibility	:	16

Manpower development

About 40,000 persons are proposed to be trained during 1998-99. Details of the personnel trained during April 1998 to December, 1 998 and the number of persons likely to be trained between January, 1999 to March, 1999 are as under:-

Courses	*No. of persons trained during April'98- Dec.'98*	*No. of persons anticipated to be trained during Jan. March 1999*	*Total*
i) Induction Courses	10651	2000	12651
ii) Inservice Courses	23578	4000	27578
iii) Courses for			

(a) Non-Departmental persons	50	30	80
(b) Foreigners	34	5	39
Total trained in departmental Training Centres	34313	6035	40348
iv) Trained abroad	53	20	73
v) Trained in India in various other institutions	36	15	51

Rural development

During the year 1998-.9, 10,941 new villages have been covered for the period from 1.4.98 to 31,12.98 against a target of 45,000 villages. It is hoped that further achievement will be made in the remaining three months to achieve the target.

New Technologies such as Wireless in Local Loop (WILL), Macro Cellular, C-DOT TDMA PMP (after successful completion of the trial of 25 systems ordered on M/s ITI), satellite based VPTs will be introduced from the year 1999-2000. Tenders have been floated for the procurement of WLL system.

Tribal Sub-Plan and N.E. Region

Tribal Sub-Plan Under 20 Points Programme

Important achievement during the period from 1st April,1998 to 31st December, 98 under Tribal Sub Plan are:

- Commissioning of 35 New Telephone Exchanges.
- Addition of 84076 Lines of Switching Capacity.
- Addition of 76101 Lines of Direct Exchange Lines.
- Commissioning of 1339 Village Telephones.
- Commissioning of 86 STD Stations.

- Commissioning of 31 UHF/Microwave/OFC schemes with 480.95 RKMs.

Development of telecom in N.E. region

Important achievements in N.E. Region during the period from 1st April, 1998 to 31st December, 98.

- Addition of 26,812 lines of switching capacity.
- Addition of 30,115 Direct Exchange lines.
- Opening of 480 Telephones in Villages.
- Opening of 14 Nos. of New Exchanges.

International co-operations/seminars/meetings

Bilateral cooperation meetings

Joint Working Group/Joint Working Commission & Inter-Ministerial Meetings.

Bilateral Co-operation meetings held in various Ministries were attended during lst April to 31 st December, 98 as detailed below:-

Meeting with H. E. H RISTO MI HAI LOVSKI the Bulgarian Deputy Minister of Trade and Tourism alongwith on official and business delegation on 28.4.98 to discuss the issues of Bilateral Co-operation.

Inter-Ministerial Meeting in connection with preliminary round of talks preceding to the next session of the Indo-Libyan Joint Commission held on 28.5.98.

Inter-Ministerial Meeting in connection with 1st Meeting of the Indo-Belarus Inter Govt. Commission on Economic, Trade, Industrial, Scientific, Technological and Cultural Co-operation held on 10.6.98.

Inter-Ministerial Meeting in connection with the next session of Indo-Belgium Joint Commission held on 11.6.98.

Inter-Ministerial Meeting in connection with 1st meeting of Joint Trade committee between India &

Zimbabwe held on 17.7.98. Indo-Zimbabwe Joint Trade Committee Meeting held in Harare on 18th & 19th August 1998 with DOT participation of a business delegation.

Inter-Ministerial Meeting in connection with the third session of the Indo-Czech Joint Committee on Trade & Economic Co-operation and third session of Indo-Slovak Joint Committee on Trade & Economic Co-operation held on 25.8.98.

Inter-Ministerial meeting held in MEA on 26.8.98 to consider the Agenda items for 12th session of the Indo-Iraq Joint Commission meeting.

Inter Ministerial meeting in connection with third meeting of Indo-Cyprus Joint Economic Meeting held on 31.8.98.

Xlth Indo-Bhutan Telecom operational co-ordination meeting held on 14th & 15th September, 1998 in Thimpu (Bhutan).

Indo-Nepal Telecom operational co-ordination meeting held on 24th & 25th September, 1998 in New Delhi.

Inter-Ministerial Meeting to finalise the Agenda for discussion with the New-Zealand side for the review Meeting of India & New-Zealand JTC held on 6.10.98.

A preparatory meeting to discuss the Agenda for the first meeting of the India-Korea Joint Commission held on 6.10.98.

A preparatory meeting held on 7.10.98 to finalise the Agenda for the Joint Trade Committee (JTC) meeting between India & Kenya.

A Mid-Term review meeting of the India & New-Zealand Joint Trade Committee was held on 13.10.98.

An Inter-Ministerial preparatory meeting for the second session of Indo-Israei Joint Trade & Economic Committee was held on 16.10.98.

An Inter-Ministerial Meeting for finalisation of brief for the Indian delegation to Indo-EC Sub-Commission was held on 16.10.98.

A preparatory meeting in connection with the forthcoming visit of official delegation led by Commerce Secretary to Yangon(Myanmar) to discuss the present status was held on 23.10.98.

The Second meeting of the Indo-Israel Joint Trade and Economic Committee was held in New Delhi on 27.10.98.

An Inter-Ministerial preparatory meeting in connection with Fourth session of the Indo Croatia Joint Committee on Trade & Economic Cooperation was held on 2.11.98.

An Inter-Ministerial meeting to finalise the Agenda for the session of Indo-French Joint Committee was held on 2.11.98.

An Inter-Ministerial meeting in connection with Fourth session of the Indo-Greek Joint Economic Committee was held on 3.11.98.

An Inter-Ministerial preparatory meeting in connection with the Commerce Secretary level discussions between India and Pakistan on "Economic Cooperation" was held on 2.11.98.

A meeting on Economic and Commercial Cooperation between India and Pakistan at Commerce Secretary level was held on 10.11.98.

First meeting on Joint Project Steering Group in connection with CIDA assisted Telecom. Frame work project was held on 11.11.98.

The third meeting of the Indo-Kenya Joint Trade Committee was held at New Delhi on 11.11.98.

An Inter-Ministerial meeting on account of the third meeting of the Indo-South African Joint Commission was held on 13.11.98.

An inter-Ministerial meeting in connection with XIIIth session of Indo-italian Joint Commission was held on 18.11.98.

9th session of Indo-French Joint Committee held in New Delhi on 23-24th November, 1998.

An Inter-Ministerial meeting to finalise the issues to be taken up during XIIIth session of the Indo-Romania Joint Commission meeting was held on 26.11.98.

An Inter-Ministerial preparatory meeting was held on 1.12.98 in connection with 10th session of the Indo-Iran Joint Commission.

Meeting on CIDA Assisted Telecom. Operation Project was held on 4.12.98.

A meeting to review the implementation of decisions taken during 9th session of Indo-fran Joint Commission by the Committee on Transport and Communication was held on 10. 12.98.

An Inter-Ministerial meeting was held on 16.12.98 in connection with Commerce Minister visit to Tanzania.

An Inter-Ministerial meeting in connection with the first meeting of Joint Trade Committee(JTC) between India & Zambia held on 16.12.98.

An Inter-Ministerial meeting held on 23.12.98 to finalise the Agenda for the Indo-EC Joint Commission.

Visit of Foreign Ministries and other dignitaries to Department of Telecom.

Mr. NORIMASA HOUSE GAWA, Vice-Minister for International Affairs. Ministry of Posts & Telecommunications, Japan called on Chairman (TC) & Hon'ble Minister of State for Communications on 24.9.98.

H.E. Mr. AHMET DENIZON GUN, Minister of Transport Communications, Turkey, alongwith Mr. YUSUF BULG, Ambassador of Turkey in New Delhi, called on Hon'ble Minister of State for Communications on 10. 12.98.

H.E. Mr. JAY NAIDOO, Minister for Posts & Telecommunications & Broadcasting South Africa called Hon'ble Minister of State for Communications on 9.12.98.

Russian Ambassador, Embassy of Russia, New Delhi made a courtesy call on Hon'ble Minister of Communication on 18.12.98.

MOU signed

An MOU between India & South Africa in the field of Telecommunications was signed on 9.12.98.

Agreement between the Govt. of the Republic of India & the Govt. of the Russian Federation on Co-operation in the field of Communications was signed on 21.12.98.

Joint Working Committee/Working Group constituted for the implementation of following MOUs between India and the following countries:-

i) Tanzabua ii) Belarus iii) Germany iv) France v) Canada, CIDA assisted projects i.e. Framework & operation.

Seminars/workshops/Meeting

The event was organised by International Telecom Union (ITU) in Johannesburg, South Africa during May 4-9,1998. Telecom: units from India, namely, MTNL, VSNL, ITI,

HTL,TCIL, Telecom Factories, C-DOT in public sector and Tata Telecom. from private sector as well as Department of Electronics participated alongwith Department of Telecommunications under the banner of India Pavilion. The pavilion was visited by large number of businessmen and official visitors including many important dignatories; Minister of Communications, South Africa, Ethiopia and Mauritius as well as Secretary General of ITU. Number of important meetings were also arranged between Indian companies and South African businessmen community.

A delegation of senior officials from DOT visited the exhibition and participated in the Seminar organised by ITU. Chairman(TC), Mr. A.V.Gokak, had a meeting with Mr.J.Naidoo, Minister of Posts & Telecommunications, South Africa.

India Tech '98 at Nairobi, Kenya during 1-4 Sept., 1998: DOT, MTNL, HTL, ITI, C-DOT and Telecom Factories participated successfully under the banner of "Telecommunications". The participation in the exhibition over four days was quite successful. The response was overwhelming from visitors, government functionaries and businessmen and in all, approximately 1200-1400 visitors came to various booths set up by telecom. units.

The dignitaries who visited are as under:

i) Hon'ble Minister of Transport & Telecommunications, Mr. Nitimama.

ii) Deputy Minister of Transport & Telecommunications, Mr.Obure.

iii) Hon'ble Minister of Industrial Development, Mr. Masakhalia.

iv) Hon'ble Asstt. Minister of Finance, Mr. Muathaias Keah.

v) Executive Chairman of Investment Promotion Centre, Dr.N.Gok.

vi) Senior Government officials/officials of Ministry of Defence & Industry Chambers.

vii) Number of Ambassadors and High Commissioners.

viii) Representative of Banking Institutions.

Second SAARC Trade Fair in Colombo (Sri Lanka) from 8-15 September, 1 998 organised by India Trade Promotion Organisation (ITPO). M/s. HTL Ltd. and M/s. TCIL participated.

National

IITF '98:- It was held during 14-27, November, 1998. Department of Telecommunications,

Department of Posts, MTNL, VSNL, TCIL, HTL, C-DOT and HCL participated successfully under the banner of "Communications". The pavilion received award for excellence.

International Relations

Deputation of officers to foreign countries for the period April'98 to December, 1998 is as follows:

i) Deputation of 21 officers to Geneva, Jersey (U.K.), Johannesburg (S.A.) and Maldives for attending meetings on different study Groups of ITU-T, ITU-R, WTO India's Trade Policy review, African Telecom. '98. Radio Communication Bureau and Regional Tariff Groups.

ii) Deputation of 16 officers to Washington, Minneapolis(USA), Manila and Bangkok for attending meetings on different study groups of APT, Business colloquium, Plenipotentiary, Inter-Active medical curriculum, Development Information Infrastructure in Rural Areas & World Economic Development Congress.

iii) Deputation of 8 officers to Tampere (Finland), Manila, Tunisjunisia), Netherland and Pretoria (South Africa) for attending different meetings/ conference on ICET'98, user supplier EWSD switch, Africa one, improving electricity efficiency in commercial buildings and Regional workshop on year 2000 (Problems on Telecommunications).

iv) Deputation of 22 officers to Seoul (Korea), Bhutan, Paris (France) & Kansai (Japan) for attending meetings of APSCC, CDMA Training programme, APII, Indo-Bangladesh link & infrastructure conference.

v) The 15th Plenipotentiary Conference of the International Telecommunication Union (ITU) was held at Minneapolis (USA) from 12 October to 6 November 1998. A high level inter-departmental Indian delegation, led by the Hon'ble MOS(C) participated in the Conference. The Conference was attended by more than 1600 delegates and participants from 170 countries and 98 from International Telecom Organisation.

Anticipated achievements

Bilateral cooperation

Joint Working Group is to be constituted for the implementation of MOU signed between India & South Africa.

Exhibition & seminar

a) International:- CEBIT '98 at Hanover, 18-24 March, 1999. Participation of M/s. VSNL has been approved. A delegation from Deptt. of Telecom. is also likely to participate.

b) National:- Sunderban Mela'99 at Canning Town, South 24 Parganas, West Bengal from 3rd January to 12th January,1999 organised by Bandhu Mahal.

Chief General Manager, West Bengal Telecom Circle, Calcutta has been requested to participate.

International relations

About 37 officers are expected for attending different seminars/conferences etc. abroad from January'99 to March'99 as mentioned below:

Activity	*No. of Officers*	
ITU-T/ITU-R/ITU-D	20	
APT Meetings/Seminars	4	
APSCC Meetings/Seminars/Workshop		1
INTELSAVINMARSAT Meetings 1		
Meetings/Workshop/Consultancies with UNDP/ITU Projects	3	
Other misc. International Activities		8
	Total :	37

Meeting and Seminar of Telecommunication Management Network (TMN), Expert Group of ITU, held on 6-15 January'99 at Bangalore.

Telecom Factories

Department of Telecommunication has seven Departmental Telecom. Factories.

Total turn over of Telecom. Factories during the year 1997-98 was 188.49 Crores against the target of Rs.198 Crores. The Financial and Quatitative achievement upto December 1998 and expected achievement upto March 1999 during the current year is indicated as under:

Financial

(Rs. in Crore)

S.N.	*Telecom Factory 1998-99*	*Target*	*Achievement from April-Dec'98*	*Expected achievement upto March'99*
i.	Mumbai	55.00	30.95	48.00

ii.	Calcutta & Gopalpur	70.00	48.34	70.00
iii.	Kharagpur	5.00	1.82	3.00
iv.	Jabalpur	65.00	45.21	65.00
v.	Richhai	35.00	15.38	25.00
vi.	Bhilai	12.00	8.03	12.00
	Total	242.00	149.73	223.00

Physical

S.N.	Item	Annual target 98-99	Achievement from April-Dec'98	Expected achievement upto March'99
i.	Bkt Ch.Ir4W	1300000	863500	1300000
ii.	Buttenski Telephone	10000	2800	4600
iii.	CBT-95	12000	4043	7000
iv.	CD Cabinets	16500	11064	15900
V.	CT Box 100 pair	150000	99470	150000
vi.	DP Boxes	500000	205627	358037
vii.	Line Jack Unit	2400000	1389700	2000000
viii.	Mast 15M	12000	5917	10000
ix.	Mast 40M	300	131	200
X.	MDF C-DOT	3500	2229	3500
xi.	Modems	1500	460	700
xii.	MW Tower (in MT)	8000	4620	8000
xiii.	Saddles	1000000	37275	40000
xiv.	Socket B	40000	25000	40000
xv.	Sole Plate	200000	85	500
xvi.	Stalks	800000	330000	550000
xvii.	Support Bkt.	1500000	563000	800000
xviii.	Tube B-8	785000	492385	800000
xix.	U-Back	1750000	703000	1200000

Telecom factories also participated in following major exhibition during the Year 1998-99

Africa Telecom'98 from 4th to 10th May,1998 in Johannesburg, South Africa.

India Industrial & Electronics Technology Exposition 1998 from 1st to 4th September 1998 in Nairobi, Kenya.

India International Trade Fair 1998 from 14-27 November 1998 at Pragariti Maidan, New Delhi.

Status of cag paras

During the year 1998-99 (upto 15.1.99) the Budget-II Section of DOT(HQ) attended to various coordination activities relating to Draft Audit Paragraphs, Audit Reports and PAC/COPU cases pertaining to the Department, besides other works indicated below.

Draft Audit Paragraphs covering P&T as well as Commercial Audit.

157 C&AG's (Union Govt.) Report on DOT for 1996-97, containing 40 paragraphs involving 163 Action Taken Notes and C&AG's (Commercial) Reports for 1996-97 containing 3 paragraphs involving 21 Action Taken Notes.

Lists of Questions on seven paragraphs selected by the PAC of Lok Sabha from C&AG's (Union Govt.) Reports on DOT for detailed examination during 1998-99. In three of these, oral evidence of the Secretary, DOT was also taken by the PAC.

Sitting of Lok Sabha's Committee on Public Sector Undertakings (COPU) on 21.12.98 for discussing with the Secretary, DOT. The follow up action taken by the department on C&AG's (Commercial) Reports.

Visits of the PAC on 9.11.98 to Patna and on 16.1.99 to Cochin for on the spot study of paragraphs of C&AG's Report (P&T) No. 6 of 1998 relating to Bihar and Kerala Telecom. Circles respectively

Review of IFAs Quarterly Reports received from field units.

Review of Quarterly statements of Audit Inspection Reports and Audit Objections received from field units.

Industrial assistance and export promotion group

During the new Industrial Policy period(01 .08.91 to 31.08.98) 452 Foreign Collaborations (106 technical and 346 financial) have been approved. During this period a total of Rs. 31466.12 crores of Foreign Direct Investment (FDI) has been approved for Telecom. sector which accounts for 18.15% of FDI approved by the Government of India.

Total production of telecom equipment and cables during 1997-98 was Rs.9960 crores. It is estimated the production would register healthy growth this year.

Private Investment Promotion Cell has been created to encourage, stimulate and facilitate private investment in telecom. sector and to smoothen the implementation of these projects.

Activities of industrial assistance and export promotion group

The Industrial Assistance and Export Promotion Group of Production Wing of DoT is responsible for the development and regulation of the Telecom Industry in the country. The main activities of the Group are:

Providing assistance in formulation of Import and Export policies for the Telecom Sector.

Providing assistance in formulation of foreign investment policies and procedures for the Telecom Sector.

Processing of applications for foreign investment and foreign technology in Telecom. Sector.

Matters relating to promotion of Telecom Exports including sponsoring of trade delegation, setting up of Indian pavilions in international Exhibition and Organisation of Seminars etc.

Assistance in matters relating to Customs and Excise

duties and other Direct and Indirect Taxes for the Telecom Sector.

Assistance in matters relating to Trade and Industrial policies for the Telecom Sector.

Assistance to various industrial units in the Telecom Sector for implementation of their projects.

Activities of private investment promotion cell

This group has been created to encourage, stimulate and facilitate private investment in telecom sector and to smoothen the implementation of these projects. Main activities of this group are:

Promotional activities

Interaction with Business Councils/industry Associations.

Interaction with Indian Investment Centre and other Govern me nt/Sem i-Government bodies concerned with investment promotion.

To recommend formation of policies to catalyse and stimulate private investment in Telecom. Sector.

Printing of Promotional Literature and their distribution.

Organisation of Investment Conferences/Seminars/ Exhibitions and dissemination of information, arrange publicity about avenues/scopes of private investment in telecom sector.

Deputation of officers from DoT for attending the National/International Conferences/ Seminars/ Exhibitions concerned with investment promotion.

Follows up action on the following issues relating to project implementation

Issues which are to be resolved within Telecom. Commission.

Issues to be resolved with other Government, Ministries, State Governments and other concerned agencies.

Issues related to VSNL/MTNL/DOT connectivity to be provided to private operators.

Issues related to foreign collaborations and other concerned approvals.

Any other problem coming in way of implementation of private telecom projects.

Financial review

The budget and revised estimate for 1998-99 and the budget estimates for the year 1999-2000 are as follows:

(Rs.in Crores)

	B. E. 1998-1999	R.E. 1998-1999	B.E. 1999-2000
Revenue Receipts	17142.13	17508:42	19788.20
Working Expenses (net)	10369.45	10256.59	10656.87
Net Receipts	6772.68	7251.83	9131.33
Divided to General Revenue	286.50	211.88	291.11
Surplus	6486.18	6969.45	8840.22
Appropriation of Surplus			
Capital Reserve Fund	6398.68	6854.50	8735.22
Revenue Reserve Fund	87.50	115.40	105.00

Tariffs

Introduction of Clip Facility and fixation of Tariff there of issued vide order No. 3-2/98-R&C dated 11.8.98.

Rebate in installation charges in respect of new telephone connections issued vide order No. 320/98-R&C dated 11. 12.98.

General

The composition of telecom commission (full time members) during 1998-99 is as follows:

Chairman	Shri A.V.Gokak	W.E.F. 4.11.96 to 28.8.98
	Shri Anil Kumar	
Member(Finance)	Shri A.Prasad	W. E. F. 31.7.97
Member(Production)	Shri R.R.N.Prasad	W.E.F. 1.10.97 to 14.1.99 (Vacant W. E. F. 15.1-99)
Member(Services)	Shri P.S.Saran	W.E.F. 11.1.95
Member(Technology)	Shri N.K.Sinha	W.E.F. 15.11.95

Use of Hindi

Acquainted all the Telecom. Circles/Administrative Off ices/Undertakings with the O.L. Act, Rules and instructions issued thereunder for their compliance for achieving the targets fixed by O.L. Department in their Annual Programme for the year under report.

Reviewed the Quarterly Progress Report regarding progressive use of Hindi received from all the Sections of DOT(Hq.) and all the Telecom. Circles/other Administrative Offices/Undertakings etc. and took necessary corrective measures in respect of those wherein defects were noticed.

Provided Hindi information through Hindi Vishesh Seva (177) and monitored thereof. This service has been extended by the Department in 30 cities.

Arranged nomination for Hindi training for those officers/officials who had not acquired working knowledge of Hindi. Similarly, Stenographers/Typists who had not undergone training in Hindi Stenography/ Typing were nominated for the above respective training courses.

Carried out inspections of Telecom. Circles/ Administrative Offices/Undertakings to ensure as to what extent the provisions of O.L. Act/Rules and instructions issued thereunder are adhered to. About 7 inspections were carried out during the year under review.

As usual Hindi Fortnight was organised from 01.09.98 to 15.09.98 which is a regular activity of every year prescribed by Deptt. of Official Language.

O.L. Branch works as a Co-ordinator from D.O.T. (Hq.) during the course of inspection of circles etc. by Committees of Parliament on Official Language which is also a regular feature every year. About 4 inspections were carried out by Committee of Parliament on Official Language during 199798. Parliamentary Committee also inspected D.O.T(H.Q) during the year under report.

Translated all the documents in Hindi/English specified in section 3 (3) of Official Language Act 1963 and Official Language Rule 1976, all the papers/reports to be laid by DOT on the table in both the Houses of Parliament.

Quarterly meetings of the Departmental Official Language Implementation Committee were held at regular interval during the period under review.

Two days Hindi Workshop was conducted in D.O.T. (H.Q) to remove the hesitation of officials in doing their daily official work in Hindi.

Akhil Bhartiya Rajbhasha Sammelan were organised in various Circle offices.

Out of minimum 10 inspection prescribed by the Department of Official Language during the year 7 inspections have been made so far remaining three inspections are to be carried out during this period.

As per programme received so far, the Committee of

Parliament on Official Language is expected to carry out 4 inspections of field offices of D.O.T. during this period.

Arranged nomination for Hindi Stenography/ Typing training of those Stenographers/Typists who had not acquired working knowledge of Hindi Stenography/ Typing for the Session starting from February, 1999.

Deputations/delegations abroad

I. No. of deputations/delegations of Govt. Officers abroad approved for attending conferences,Seminars, Inspections and Trainings etc. (excluding deputations/delegations sponsored under Colombo Plan UNDP Technical Assistance Programme for the year 1998-99 (upto 31.12.98).	No. of Officials included in deputation/ delegations	Estimated expenditure sanctioned (Rs. in lakhs)
96	155	170.95

II. No. of projects estimates/ Expenditure Finance Committee Memo. for construction of Telephone Exchange Buildings Installation of Telephone Exchange/ Satellite Earth/ Co-axial/MW/UHF-VFT/ Railway Electrification Scheme etc. sanctioned during the period from 1.4.98 to 31.12.98	No. of PEs	Total estimated capital expenditure. (Rs. in Crores)	Remarks (2) CTB under consider-tion
Remunerative PEs	—	—	—
Anticipated achievement & developments for the period ending 1.1.99 to 31.3.99	5	80	CTB

Work study and EB and inspection

Actual Achievements (from 1.4.98 to 31.12.98)

52 Norms Studies in respect of STS cadre in Telecom. Wing have been completed.

5 Work Measurement studies of the Headquarters have been completed.

Administrative Inspection of 5 circle offices have been completed and 1 Heads of Telecom. Circles conference was convened on 17.9.98 and minutes issued on 27th Oct. 98.

Anticipated achievements and developments (from 1.1.99 to 31.3.99):

Norms Studies in respect of STS Cadre in Telecom. Wing and 1 Norms Study in respect of Accounts personnel in SSAs is expected to be completed.

3 Work Measurement Studies in Headquarters are expected to be completed.

Welfare and sports

An amount of about Rs 4 crores has been provided to the Welfare and Sports activities to the Department of Telecommunications during the year 1998. An amount of Rs.3,26,64,982/- has been disbursed to different circles/ units for meeting their Welfare and Sports expenditure from 1st April, 1998 to 31 st December, 1998.

The following important schemes for grant of financial assistance from Welfare fund to the Telecom. employees or their dependents have been formulated and are being enjoyed by our employees and their dependents as the case may be.

(a) Financial assistance to the dependents of deceased employees.

(b) Supply of sewing machines to the families of deceased employees.

(c) Financial assistance in cases of death of casual labourers (temporary status mazdoor); in cases of death of retired employees; in prolonged illness cases of employees; in serious illness/major operations etc; on account of prolonged illness of the dependents of employees; for nutritive diet for TB patients; by way of loans in emergency cases; to victims of natural calamities; to handicapped for purchase of artificial limb centre; to handicapped children on account of transport/hostel/mess charges; towards railway fares from headquarters to Artificial limb centre.

(d) Scholarships and awards.

(e) Book awards and incentives to meritorious childrens.

(f) Grant-in-aid to Recreation/sports club.

(q) Holiday excursion trips.

There is Telecom. Women's Central Organisation (TWCO) for undertaking Welfare activities for Telecom. Women and their children which includes opening of creches, tailoring centres, nursery school and arts and crafts classes. The annual grant to TWCO is Rs.2 lakhs (and for its branches located in circles is to Rs. 15,000/-). Creches can now be opened in both office buildings or in Colonies depending upon the consensus and convenience of the user employees. In any cases building would not be rented specifically for this purposes.

Out of 36 holiday homes at present functioning in the important hill stations/health resorts, 14 are under administrative control of Department of Telecom. These are utilised by the employees of Department for holidaying purpose.

To develop Sports among Sportsmen, tournaments in 17 disciplines were conducted at different places on all India basis. An amount of Rs.83,52,500/- was spent for Sports and Cultural activities upto December 1998.

P&T Sports Control Board has sent combined P&T

teams for Nationals in the Power lifting, Weightlifting, Chess, Wrestling and kabaddi tournaments upto 31st Dec.,1998. We have spent Rs.76,482/- for sending teams for National tournaments. For improving standard of Sports in the Department, 4 sports have been selected for special development and achieving excellences.

Vigilance

Highlights of important vigilance activities during the period (1.4.98 - 31.12.98)

(i)	No. of vigilance complaints on which action completed		:	2883
(ii)	No. of Officers suspended			
		G.O.	:	14
		N.G.O.	:	48
(iii)	No. of Officers charge sheeted for			
	(a) Major penalty			
		G.O.	:	110
		N.G.O.	:	116
	(b) Minor penalty			
		G.O.	:	85
		N.G.O.	:	186
(iv)	No. of Officers punished with			
	(a) Major penalty			
		G.O.	:	50
		N.G.O.	:	42
	(b) Minor penalty			
		G.O.	:	81
		N.G.O.	:	85
(v)	No. of Officers prosecuted			
		G.O.	:	11
		N.G.O.	:	36

Training

Vigilance Officers' Conference at ALTTC, Ghaziabad was organised in December,1998 in which 60 Officers from all the telecom circles participated. The participants were informed about techniques of investigation, framing of chargesheets, store management and avoidance of frauds in high tech areas. Two more vigilance courses are proposed to be organised at Hyderabad and Chennai in March, 1999.

Other training

Other activities

Special CBI Cells set up in metro cities to prevent leakage of telecom revenue continued to perform well and gave encouraging results. Though it is not possible to quantify their gains in concrete financial terms, these cells have registered 140 cases involving 157 Departmental officials and 35 outsiders.

Special squads

Special Squads were formed in the year 1995 for surprise visits to the subscribers' premises and Telephone exchanges. The main job of these squads is random checking of equipments, telephone lines etc. to find out tampering, if any, with the equipments or lines in the switch room/external plant. Follow up action was taken on various irregularities/omissions found by the special squads. This has resulted in considerable improvement in the services and preventing misuse of lines.

Technical solutions

A committee of technical experts was constituted to examine the technical aspects involved in the matter of revenue loss caused by long duration ISD unbilled calls. The committee has made various valuable recommendations like uniformly sending CLI alongwith station code from exchanges, no access for ISD from analogue exchanges, serving ISD subscribers from CLI supporting exchanges, use of CCS #7 signalling for preventing sample monitoring of ISD calls from VSNL, spare NEND checking, taking threshold printouts and making sample checks and investigation of long duration

ISD calls. Instructions to the field units for implementation of these recommendations are being issued by the concerned authorities in the DoT headquarters.

Further, a core group of experts under the chairmanship of DDG(SW), TEC has been constituted vide order dated 30.10.98 to examine and identify the areas in the new technology systems (both switching and transmission) having scope for possible frauds leading to loss of revenue and to suggest remedial measures to prevent possibility of such incidences. The report since submitted by the Committee is under examination.

A Committee was set up under the Chairmanship of GM(Vig.), MTNL, New Delhi to study the proposal for establishment of a Fraud Management & Control Centre on experimental basis. The report submitted by the Committee is under examination.

Economic Research Unit & Statistical Section

The following studies/exercises have been undertaken/ completed during the year 1998-99:-

Impact of Group Dialling Scheme on Revenue.

Operating Ratio and rate of Return in Telecom distt.

Traffic Pattern of STID PCOs.

Economics Viability of VPTs.

Telephone Revenue - An Analysis of Trends and An Examination of Determinants for 199596 and 1996-97.

Call Slab Wise Distribution Pattern of Subscribe rs/ Calls - A case study of 8/28 Telecom, District: 1995-96 and 1996-97.

Downfall in Average Revenue per DEL in Tamil Nadu Telecom. Circle.

Indian Telecommunication Statistics - 1997.

Impact of Rural Tariff on Calling Pattern, Demand Sensitivity and the loss due to subsidy.

Reduction in Average Revenue per DEL and its correlation with Metered Call Unit per DEL.

Impact of the present Four-tier tariff structure and policy of dimensioning of long distance circuits on Revenue per DEL.

Composite publication of DOT for wider circulation amongst public/consumer business.

Telephone Demand Projections - Towns having exchanges with 200 lines and above 1999 -2009.

Survey to ascertain the social background and income strata of PCOs/telephone users.

Electrical Wing

The Electrical Wing of the Department of Telecom. is providing supporting services to the Telecom Network and is mainly responsible for providing all the Electrical and Electromechanical Services like Building Electrification, A.C. Plants, stand by Generating Sets, Sub Stations, Fire Fighting and Fire Detection systems etc. in the Telecom. Technical and Administrative buildings and Staff Quarters of the Department of Telecom.

In physical terms our contribution for the year 1998-99 is as under:

Year	Air Conditioning	Sub Stations	Stand by Gen. Sets
From 1.4.98 to 31.12.98	17,943 TR	61,015 KVA	1,25,690 KVA
Proposed from 1.1.99 to 31.3.99	19,000 TR	83,000 KVA	1,28,000 KVA

In financial terms our budget for the year 1998-99 is Rs.400 crores.

Review of rules and procedures

An expert group under the Chairmanship of Shri

R.N.Goyal, Advisor(HRD) reviewed the telecom. service procedures governing the customer services to make them more customer friendly.

Indian Telegraph Rules 1951 have been updated till August 1998.

Indian Telegraph Act 1885, Indian Telegraph Rules 1951, TRAI Act 1997 and Indian Wireless Telegraphy Act 1933 have been documented in the form of a compendium in billingual form. The document is awaiting printing.

Telecom Quality Assurance

Value of stores accepted upto December 1998 : Rs.3501 Crores.

(a) No. of QA Centres Opened: One at the premises of M/s. Fine Cable Industries, Madurai,

(b) No. of QA Centres closed : Four located at M/s. L&T, Mysore, M/s. Udaya Semiconductors, Coimbatore, M/s. KTL, Bangalore, M/s. Amco, Bangalore; depending upon the shift in DoTs ROs,

No. of Infrastructure Assessments carried out: 136.

(a) Conventional Products - 50

(b) TEC Products - 86

(c) No. of Type Approval Certificates issued: 304

(d) No. of Type Approval Certificates withdrawn : Nil.

No. of important meetings held: 25

(a) User's Meet: 17

(b) Others : 8

No. of First Product Qualification Cases

No. of Major Quality Problems settled

a) No. of AIS accorded : 5 including 4 extensions

(b) No. of DIS accorded: 7 including 6 extensions

Total working strength of QA Circle is reduced to 743.

Component Approval Centre for Telecommunications (CACT):

(a) Augmentation of test facility

- An instrument CAVIDERM Model CD 8 was procured from M/s UPA Technology, USA and installed in PCB lab. of CACT, Bangalore for measurement of plated through hole of copper plating thickness of double sided & multilayer PCBs.
- Test Programmes were developed for testing 22 new components viz., (a) 4-ICs (b) 9-Transistors & (c) 9-Diodes.
- Solvent Resistance Test Machine, Accelerated Ageing machine have been procured and installed in PCB Lab.
- Three Terminal Test Cell with heater has been procured in FA Lab. to test Cable Filling Compound.
- Bulk Density Apparatus for testing PVC Resin addle d in FA Lab.
- UV light source is installed to verify uniformity of conformal coating.

(b) Activity:

- No. of Components Type Approved: 358
- No. of components manufacturer's infrastructure assessed : 25
- No. of components tested in various laboratories : 14198
- No. of products subjected to climatic and environmental tests

  (i) Equipments 1884

(ii) Components 290

(iii) Others 58

- Total climatic chamber hours utilised : 20819
- No. of devices subjected to Failure Analysis : 511
- Failure Analysis reports will be released progressively.
- No. of reports generated by SCRAM : 26

Important feedback cases settled

- There was a complaint from OTC, Lucknow, OTC Project, Allahabad and OTC (Installed), Hyderabad on 8 Mbps OLTE of M/s. MAC, Bangalore supplied by M/s. Natelco, Nasik.
- The system failed in stability test after installation and even in local loop test also. The failures were noticed at different time intervals in different systems.
- The problem was analysed by M/s. MAC, Bangalore (technology provider) and finally software was modified for E-2 supervisory card. The manufacturer has changed all EPROM with modified software in all existing system (258 Nos.) which were already supplied and installed. All systems with modified EPROM are performing well and no further complaints.
- There was a feed back report from Gujarat, Karnataka besides one or two other circles on EPBT instruments supplied by M/s. Webel, Calcutta.
- The instruments failed in field during warranty in the range of 0.5 to 1.5% of the total numbers supplied. The problem was noticed in earlier batches supplied.
- Proper investigations were carried out and necessary

corrective and preventive actions were taken besides attending to the field problems by M/s. Webel for repair or replacement of the instruments.

- There was a feed back case from CTS Lucknow and CTS Bhopal on 2/15 MARR Systems supplied by M/s. HTL, Chennai-32.
- Packing cases damaged and packing note not tallying with the ICs at Lucknow and packing cases damaged at Bhopal.
- It was observed by the field unit at Lucknow that there was no damage to the equipments even though almost all packing cases containing BSU, BSUs and feeder cables were damaged. Further the packing note was not tallying with the ICs due to inadvertent despatch of the system by M/s., HTL. The firm was advised to be more careful in future to avoid such discrepancies.
- M/s. HTL visited the site at Bhopal during August 1998 and observed that there was no damage to the equipment.
- However the firm was advised to improve the packing. Accordingly M/s. HTL has improved packing by reinforcing the packing boxes by providing three steel bands over the shook boxes. Also the RP cables for RSUs are being packed separately in wooden boxes to avoid damages. Further the thickness of ply is increased from 3mm to 6mm.
- OPC Project, Hyderabad has made a complaint on 12P OP Cable supplied by M/s. Sterlite Industries, Aurangabad.
- Field units encountered some difficulty in removing the outer jacket of the cable as the jelly content is found to be very less comparatively.

- It is clarified by the manufacturer that the difficulty expressed by the field units in removal of the outer jacket is due to the fact that while removing the outer jacket and sheath the polyster tape is not being cut and that for smooth and easy removal of outer jacket it is essential that the polyster tape should be cut.
- This procedure was demonstrated by the firm successfully and to the satisfaction of the field staff as per the joint inspection report.

Major Quality Problems

In C-DOT switches, 96 & 64 pins female euro connectors of ESSEN make were giving problem after 72 hours burn in test at 50 degree Centigrate some pins were coming out resulting in improper connection. The problem was set right by certain modification in manufacturing process.

- The EPBT instruments supplied by M/s. ITI encountered moisture and low insulation problem in coastal areas.
- Conformal coating on PCB has been implemented by EPBT manufacturers to overcome the above problem.
- The fault of voltage appearing on edge strip of some XEJ cards of M/s. ITI, Mankapur were rectified by modification in PCB circuit.
- There was a field complaint on 140 Mb/s OLTE and 2/34 skip mux of M/s. HPCL that the jack in & jack out problems were existing in the racks. This has been solved by re-engineering the mechanical design of rack.

Quality Control at major factories

The fault rate in C-DOT switches of M/s. HTL were observed to be more in earlier. To minimise the faults and shorten the testing time, M/s. HTL was advised to involve the same team of engineers, technical assistants right from the first stage of production till integration/ testing of the complete equipment. This was implemented by M/s. HTL in addition to performing comparative study on the four teams set up for this purpose. After the introduction of this procedure, the faults of QA testing stage have come down.

- The QA systems at M/s. ITI, Palakkad, M/s. BPL, Palakkad, M/s. Tata Telecom, Palakkad, M/s. Trace Cables, Cochin & M/s. Keltron, Trivandrum are satisfactory.
- In view of the feedback complaints from field about the self supporting drop wire as poor in quality the following steps were taken by the manufacturers.

(a) Printing the identity of the manufacturer is introduced instead of embossing and 100% inspection on pirating is carried out.

(b) The PVC should be from CACT approved sources.

(c) Tight inspection is being followed.

Important Events

Member (Tech), Telecom. Commission, New Delhi had visited Bangalore on 7.9.98 and 8.9.98. He has visited CACT lab. and had an interaction with Sr. Officers of TQA Circle and RTEC, Bangalore.

The "Sanchar Shree" award function was held in association with Karnataka Telecom Circle on 17.5.98.

The "Sanchar Sarathi" award function for southern region of Telecom Quality Assurance Circle was held at Bangalore on 20.7.98 and for northern & eastern region it was held at M/s. ITI, Naini on 24.7.98.

Seminars/training

- 19 seminars/workshops on various subjects were

conducted by Telecom. QA Circle for the benefit of its personnel.

- QA Circle also participated in Seminars/training programmes conducted by outside agencies.

UNDP project activities

- Three DoT QA Officers were deputed abroad for training in the field of software QA and Digital Transmission Equipment.
- UNDP, New Delhi authorised chartered accountant, conducted audit on the on going UNDP project at CACT, Bangalore.

World telecom day celebration

World Telecom Day was celebrated. On this occasion, GM (PIg), Calcutta Telephones delivered a lecture on Technologies Driving Telecommunications in the office of Director (QA), Calcutta.

Representatives from various industries in Calcutta and DoT (QA) officials attended the lecture. CACT Building at Bangalore was illuminated on this occasion.

Value of stores anticipated for the period from 1.1.99 to 31.3.99 : Around Rs.1500 Crores.

(a) No. of QA Centres likely to be opened : One at Jamshedpur.

(b) No. of QA Centres likely to be closed : Two located at M/s. BPL, Palakkad and M/s Keltron

Communications, Mudadi (Kozhidone Dt. Kerala)

No. of infrastructure assessments likely to be carried out : 42

(a) Conventional Products - 15

(b) TEC Products - 27

No. of type approval certificates likely to be issued : 75

No. of important meeting likely to be held : 5

(a) User's Meet:4

(b) Others : 1

No. of First Production Qualification cases likely to be completed 4

No. of major quality problems likely to be settled : 2

(a) No. of AIS likely to be accorded 5

(b) No. of DIS likely to be accorded 2

Component Approval Centre for Telecommunications (CACT)

(a) Augmentation of Test Facility :

Peel pull tester is likely to be installed.

(b) Activities :

- No. of components likely to be type approved : 98
- No. of components manufacturer's infrastructure likely to be assessed 19
- No. of components likely to be tested in various laboratories : 4300
- No. of products likely to be subjected to climate and environmental tests : 165
- Total climatic chamber hours likely to be utilised : 6600
- No. of devices likely to be subjected to failure analysis : 150
- No. of failure analysis reports likely to be released : NIL
- No. of reports likely to be generated at SCRAM : 15